NEW IDEAS FOR APPLIQUÉ

by Pat Sloan

LEISURE ARTS, INC.
Little Rock, Arkansas

EDITORIAL STAFF
Vice President of Editorial: Susan White Sullivan
Special Projects Director: Susan Frantz Wiles
Director of E-Commerce: Mark Hawkins
Art Publications Director: Rhonda Shelby
Technical Writer: Jean Lewis
Technical Associates: Frances Huddleston and
    Lisa Lancaster
Editorial Writer: Susan McManus Johnson
Art Category Manager: Lora Puls
Graphic Artists: Kara Darling, Stacy Owens,
    Becca Snider, and Amy Temple
Imaging Technician: Stephanie Johnson
Prepress Technician: Janie Marie Wright
Photography Manager: Katherine Laughlin
Contributing Photographer: Ken West
Contributing Photo Stylist: Sondra Daniel
Manager of E-Commerce: Robert Young

BUSINESS STAFF
President and Chief Executive Officer: Rick Barton
Vice President of Sales: Mike Behar
Vice President of Finance: Laticia Mull Dittrich
Director of Corporate Planning: Anne Martin
National Sales Director: Martha Adams
Creative Services: Chaska Lucas
Information Technology Director: Hermine Linz
Controller: Francis Caple
Vice President of Operations: Jim Dittrich
Retail Customer Service Manager: Stan Raynor
Vice President of Purchasing: Fred F. Pruss

Library of Congress Control Number: 2012934307

ISBN-13: 978-1-60900-425-5

Table of Contents

Meet Pat Sloan

You'll never meet a more devoted fan of the quilting arts than Pat Sloan! When she isn't designing fabric, writing quilt books, teaching quilt techniques, or developing patterns, she draws on her background as a computer programmer to maintain her popular Website and blog at PatSloan.com. Pat's joyful approach to quilting seems to be contagious, because "Sloanies" (as Pat's devoted fans call themselves) love to keep up with their favorite designer while she pursues the quilting life with a passion.

"I've been fulltime as a quilt designer and teacher since 2000," says Pat, "with my husband Gregg handling the business side of managing our company. My life is all about quilting, twenty-four/seven."

If you want to discover more of Pat's exciting designs and original quilt-making techniques, visit your local fabric store or LeisureArts.com to collect all of her books!

A Note From Pat

I inherited my love of decorating for the seasons from my Granny—she was the queen of seasonal decorating. Granny always had festive candy dishes, fabulous Easter baskets, colorful summer lawn ornaments, and her house was a legend at Christmas time!

To carry on the tradition, I designed my Year of Appliqué Quilt to feature a block for every month. The designs include flowers, a snowman, a pumpkin, an angel, and much more.

Version I, shown on pages 5 and 32, is made from fun batik fabrics for a bright and bold look. Version II, shown on page 35, uses more traditional colors and prints for a warm and toasty feel.

To make either version of this quilt, you might want to organize or participate in a block of the month group through your local quilt shop or guild, or you can opt to make it on your own from start to finish.

But don't stop with the quilt! Other seasonal projects include a tabletop set, a project bag, a pillow, and a throw. Some of the blocks can even be finished as mini quilts, like the snowman on page 66.

Whether you make the quilt, the individual projects, or both, I hope you have fun and send me pictures!

Happy Quilts Cathy! -Pat

3

a Year of Appliqué

Finished Quilt Size For Either Version: 85" x 85" (216 cm x 216 cm)

MAKING THE BLOCKS

Before You Begin:

- Fabric requirements and instructions are given individually for each of the 12 blocks.

- Version I border fabric requirements and finishing instructions begin on page 31.

- Version II border fabric requirements and finishing instructions begin on page 34.

- If you are making the Year Of Appliqué quilt and wish to purchase fabric for the entire checkerboard border, you will need $1^3/_8$ yards of cream batik and $1^3/_8$ yards of black batik fabric.

- Hot-fix crystals for "eyes" listed in fabric requirements are optional. Version I has them, Version II does not.

Version 1 shown here, Version 2 shown on page 35.

5

JANUARY: Fun in the Snow

Finished Block Size: 28" x 20" (71 cm x 51 cm)

Fabric Requirements

Yardage is based on 43"/44" (109 cm/112 cm) wide fabric with a usable width of 40" (102 cm).

Two 6^1/$_2$" x 14^1/$_2$" (17 cm x 37 cm) **rectangles** of grey batik for background

12^1/$_2$" x 14^1/$_2$" (32 cm x 37 cm) **rectangle** of blue batik for background

^{1}/$_4$ yd (23 cm) *each* of 1 cream and 1 black batik for checkerboard border *

9" x 15" (23 cm x 38 cm) rectangle of white print #1 for snowman

12" x 12" (30 cm x 30 cm) square of white print #2 for snowflakes

20" x 5" (51 cm x 13 cm) rectangle of red batik for hat

Scraps of black, orange, and brown batiks for remaining appliqués

You will also need:

1 pair of 5 mm hot-fix crystals for eyes

Paper-backed fusible web

* See Bullet #4, page 5, if making the entire quilt.

Cutting the Pieces

*Follow **Rotary Cutting**, page 76, to cut fabric. Cut all strips from the selvage-to-selvage width of the fabric. All measurements include ^{1}/$_4$" seam allowances.*

From cream batik:
- Cut 2 **strips** 2^1/$_2$" wide.

From black batik:
- Cut 2 **strips** 2^1/$_2$" wide.

Cutting the Appliqués

*Follow **Fusible Appliqué**, page 79, to make appliqués from January patterns, pages 37-39.*

From white print #1:
- Cut 1 **snowman head**.
- Cut 1 **snowman tummy**.
- Cut 1 **snowman base**.

From white print #2:
- Cut 3 **snowflakes**.
- Cut 3 **snowflake centers**.

From red batik:
- Cut 1 **hat**.

From scraps of orange, black, and brown batiks:
- Cut 1 **hatband**.
- Cut 1 **pompom**.
- Cut 1 **nose**.
- Cut 1 of *each* **arm**.

Making the Block

*Follow **Piecing** and **Pressing**, page 77. Match right sides and use a ^{1}/$_4$" seam allowance.*

1. Matching long edges, sew 2 grey **rectangles** and blue **rectangle** together to make **background**.

Background

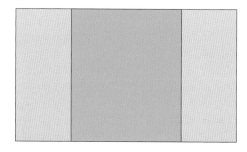

2. Referring to **Making Strip Sets**, page 77, use cream and black **strips** to make 2 **Strip Sets**. From these, cut 28 **Unit 1's**.

Unit 1 (make 28)

3. Matching short edges, sew 6 Unit 1's together to make **Unit 2**.

Unit 2

4. Matching short edges, sew 5 Unit 1's together to make **Unit 3**. Make 2 Unit 3's.

Unit 3 (make 2)

5. Matching long edges, sew 12 Unit 1's together to make **Unit 4**.

Unit 4

6. Sew Unit 2 to 1 long edge and Unit 4 to remaining long edge of background to make **Unit 5**.

Unit 5

7. Sew 1 Unit 3 to either side of Unit 5 to make **Unit 6**.

Unit 6

Adding the Appliqués

*Refer to **Blanket Stitch Appliqué**, page 79, for stitching techniques.*

1. Working from the background up, arrange **appliqués** on Unit 6; fuse.
2. Blanket Stitch around appliqués to complete **Fun In The Snow** block. **Note:** Crystal "eyes" are added to snowman after quilting project.

Fun In The Snow Block

FEBRUARY: Love Blooms

Finished Block Size: 14" x 20" (36 cm x 51 cm)

Fabric Requirements

Yardage is based on 43"/44" (109 cm/112 cm) wide fabric with a usable width of 40" (102 cm). A fat quarter is approximately 18" x 22" (46 cm x 56 cm)

- 12¹/₂" x 18¹/₂"(32 cm x 47 cm) rectangle of grey batik for **background**
- ¹/₈ yd (11 cm) *each* of 1 cream and 1 black batik for checkerboard border
- 7" x 12" (18 cm x 30 cm) rectangle of blue batik for circles
- 11" x 14" (28 cm x 36 cm) rectangle of pink batik for hearts
- 1 fat quarter of green batik for leaves and stems

You will also need:
- Fabric basting glue
- Paper-backed fusible web

Cutting the Pieces

*Follow **Rotary Cutting**, page 76, to cut fabric. Cut all strips from the selvage-to-selvage width of the fabric. All measurements include ¹/₄" seam allowances.*

From cream batik:
- • Cut 1 **strip** 2¹/₂" wide.

From black batik:
- • Cut 1 **strip** 2¹/₂" wide.

Cutting the Appliqués

*Follow **Fusible Appliqué**, page 79, to make appliqués from February patterns, pages 40-41.*

From blue batik:
- • Cut 3 **circles**.

From pink batik:
- • Cut 3 **hearts**.

From green batik:
- • Cut 1 of *each* **leaf A-C**.
- • Cut 3 *bias* **stems** ¹/₂" x 13".

Making the Block

*Follow **Piecing** and **Pressing**, page 77. Match right sides and use a ¹/₄" seam allowance.*

1. Referring to **Making Strip Sets**, page 77, use cream and black **strips** to make 1 **Strip Set**. From this, cut 8 Unit 1's.

Unit 1 (make 8)

2. Matching short edges, sew 3 Unit 1's together to make Unit 2.

Unit 2

3. Matching short edges, sew 5 Unit 1's together to make Unit 3.

Unit 3

4. Sew Unit 2 to **background** to make Unit 4.

Unit 4

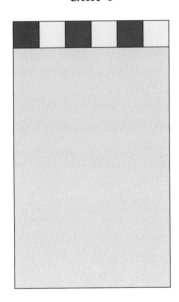

5. Sew Unit 3 to Unit 4 to make Unit 5.

Unit 5

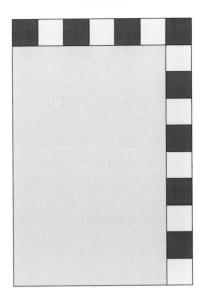

Adding the Appliqués

*Refer to **Blanket Stitch Appliqué**, page 79, for stitching techniques.*

1. Working from the background up, arrange **leaves**, **circles**, and **hearts** on Unit 5; do not fuse.
2. Trimming and tucking as needed, arrange **stems** on background; secure stems with drops of basting glue. Fuse all appliqués in place.
3. Blanket Stitch around appliqués to complete Love Blooms Block.

Love Blooms Block

MARCH: Welcome Home

Finished Block Size: 22" x 20" (56 cm x 51 cm)

Fabric Requirements

Yardage is based on 43"/44" (109 cm/112 cm) wide fabric with a usable width of 40" (102 cm).

- 16^1/$_2$" x 16^1/$_2$" (42 cm x 42 cm) square of tan batik for **background**
- ^{1}/$_4$ yd (23 cm) *each* of 1 cream and 1 black batik for checkerboard border
- 8" x 10" (20 cm x 25 cm) rectangle of black batik for birdhouse
- 7" x 9" (18 cm x 23 cm) rectangle of gold batik for roof
- 11" x 11" (28 cm x 28 cm) square of green batik #1 for leaves and stems
- 8" x 9" (20 cm x 23 cm) rectangle of green batik #2 for leaves
- Scraps of purple, orange, light orange, cream, and black batiks for remaining appliqués

You will also need:
- Paper-backed fusible web

Cutting the Pieces

*Follow **Rotary Cutting**, page 76, to cut fabric. Cut all strips from the selvage-to-selvage width of the fabric. All measurements include ^{1}/$_4$" seam allowances.*

From cream batik:
- Cut 2 **strips** 2^1/$_2$" wide.

From black batik:
- Cut 2 **strips** 2^1/$_2$" wide.

Cutting the Appliqués

*Follow **Fusible Appliqué**, page 79, to make appliqués from March patterns, pages 41-43.*

From black batik:
- Cut 1 **birdhouse**.

From gold batik:
- Cut 1 **roof**. Cut 1 **roof reversed**.

From green batik #1:
- Cut 1 **leaf**. Cut 1 **leaf reversed**.
- Cut 2 **stems**. Cut 1 **stem reversed**.

From green batik #2:
- Cut 1 **leaf**. Cut 1 **leaf reversed**.

From scraps of purple, orange, light orange, cream, and black batiks:
- Cut 1 **star**.
- Cut 3 **flowers**.
- Cut 1 **opening**.
- Cut 1 **bird**. Cut 1 **bird reversed**.
- Cut 1 **wing**. Cut 1 **wing reversed**.
- Cut 2 **eyes**.

Making the Block

*Follow **Piecing** and **Pressing**, page 77. Match right sides and use a ^{1}/$_4$" seam allowance.*

1. Referring to **Making Strip Sets**, page 77, use cream and black **strips** to make 2 **Strip Sets**. From these, cut 23 Unit 1's.

Unit 1 (make 23)

2. Matching short edges, sew 4 Unit 1's together to make Unit 2. Make 2 Unit 2's.

Unit 2 (make 2)

3. Matching short edges, sew 5 Unit 1's together to make Unit 3.

Unit 3

4. Matching long edges, sew 10 Unit 1's together to make Unit 4.

Unit 4

5. Sew 1 Unit 2 to opposite edges of **background** to make Unit 5.

Unit 5

6. Sew Unit 3 and Unit 4 to Unit 5 to make Unit 6.

Unit 6

Adding the Appliqués

Refer to **Blanket Stitch Appliqué**, *page 79, for stitching techniques.*

1. Working from the background up, arrange **appliqués** on Unit 6; fuse.
2. Blanket Stitch around appliqués to complete Welcome Home Block.

Welcome Home Block

APRIL:
Spring Breeze

Finished Block Size: 20" x 16" (51 cm x 41 cm)

Fabric Requirements
Yardage is based on 43"/44" (109 cm/112 cm) wide fabric with a usable width of 40" (102 cm).

- Two 8½" x 8½" (22 cm x 22 cm) **squares** of tan batik for background
- Two 8½" x 8½" (22 cm x 22 cm) **squares** of grey batik for background
- ⅛ yd (11 cm) *each* of 1 cream and 1 black batik for checkerboard border
- 9" x 14" (23 cm x 36 cm) rectangle of blue batik for butterfly wings
- 6" x 8" (15 cm x 20 cm) rectangle of black batik for butterfly bodies
- 6" x 6" (15 cm x 15 cm) square of hot pink batik for star
- Scraps of green, light pink, and cream batiks for remaining appliqués

You will also need:
- 4 pairs of 3 mm hot-fix crystals for eyes
- Paper-backed fusible web

Cutting the Pieces
*Follow **Rotary Cutting**, page 76, to cut fabric. Cut all strips from the selvage-to-selvage width of the fabric. All measurements include ¼" seam allowances.*

From cream batik:
- Cut 1 **strip** 2½" wide.

From black batik:
- Cut 1 **strip** 2½" wide.

Cutting the Appliqués
*Follow **Fusible Appliqué**, page 79, to make appliqués from April patterns, page 44.*

From blue batik:
- Cut 4 **large wings**.
- Cut 4 **small wings**.

From black batik:
- Cut 4 **bodies**.

From hot pink batik:
- Cut 1 **star**.

From scraps of green, light pink, and cream batiks:
- Cut 4 **flowers**.
- Cut 4 **buds**.
- Cut 4 **stems**.
- Cut 4 **leaves**.

Making the Block

*Follow **Piecing** and **Pressing**, page 77. Match right sides and use a ¹/₄" seam allowance.*

1. Sew 2 grey and 2 tan **squares** together to make **background**.

Background

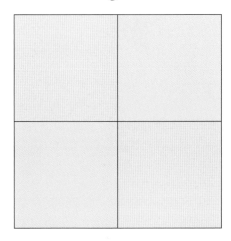

2. Referring to **Making Strip Sets**, page 77, use cream and black **strips** to make 1 **Strip Set**. From this cut 8 **Unit 1's**.

Unit 1 (make 8)

3. Matching short edges, sew 4 Unit 1's together to make **Unit 2**. Make 2 Unit 2's.

Unit 2 (make 2)

4. Sew 1 Unit 2 to opposite sides of background to make **Unit 3**.

Unit 3

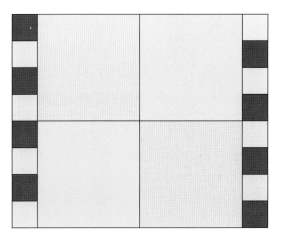

Adding the Appliqués

*Refer to **Blanket Stitch Appliqué**, page 79, for stitching techniques.*

1. Working from the background up, arrange **appliqués** on Unit 3; fuse.
2. Blanket Stitch around appliqués to complete **Spring Breeze Block** block.
   Note: Crystal "eyes" are added to dragonflies after quilting project.

Spring Breeze Block

13

MAY:
Pear Blossoms

Finished Block Size: 28" x 10" (71 cm x 25 cm)

Fabric Requirements

Yardage is based on 43"/44" (109 cm/112 cm) wide fabric with a usable width of 40" (102 cm).

- 8¹/₂" x 26¹/₂" (22 cm x 67 cm) rectangle of tan batik for **background**
- ¹/₈ yd (11 cm) *each* of 1 cream and 1 black batik for checkerboard border
- 5" x 8" (13 cm x 20 cm) rectangle *each* of 3 assorted green batiks and 1 gold batik for pears
- 8" x 14" (20 cm x 36 cm) rectangle of dark green batik for stems and leaves
- 10" x 10" (25 cm x 25 cm) square of orange batik for flowers
- Scraps of gold, black, cream, and purple batiks for remaining appliqués

You will also need:

- 2 pairs of 3 mm hot-fix crystals for eyes
- Paper-backed fusible web

Cutting the Pieces

*Follow **Rotary Cutting**, page 77, to cut fabric. Cut all strips from the selvage-to-selvage width of the fabric. All measurements include ¹/₄" seam allowances.*

From cream batik:
- Cut 1 **strip** 2¹/₂" wide.

From black batik:
- Cut 1 **strip** 2¹/₂" wide.

Cutting the Appliqués

*Follow **Fusible Appliqué**, page 79, to make appliqués from May patterns, pages 45-46.*

From assorted green and gold batiks:
- Cut 1 **large pear**.
- Cut 2 **medium pears**.
- Cut 1 **small pear**.

From dark green batik:
- Cut 5 **leaves**. Cut 1 **leaf reversed**.

From orange batik:
- Cut 3 **flowers**.
- Cut 1 **stem**.

From scraps of gold, black, cream, and purple batiks:
- Cut 2 **bees**.
- Cut 2 of *each* **stripe A-B**.
- Cut 3 **star petals**.
- Cut 2 **wings**.
- Cut 3 **flower centers**.

Making the Block

*Follow **Piecing** and **Pressing**, page 77. Match right sides and use a 1/4" seam allowance.*

1. Referring to **Making Strip Sets**, page 77, use cream and black **strips** to make 1 **Strip Set**. From this, cut 9 **Unit 1's**.

Unit 1 (make 9)

2. Matching short edges, sew 2 Unit 1's together to make Unit 2.

Unit 2

3. Matching short edges, sew 7 Unit 1's together to make Unit 3.

Unit 3

4. Sew Unit 2 to **background** to make Unit 4.

Unit 4

5. Sew Unit 3 to Unit 4 to make Unit 5.

Unit 5

Adding the Appliqués

*Refer to **Blanket Stitch Appliqué**, page 79, for stitching techniques.*

1. Working from the background up, arrange **appliqués** on Unit 5; fuse. **Note:** For appliqués that extend into the borders of adjacent blocks, leave protruding edges free.

2. Blanket Stitch around appliqués to complete Pear Blossom block. **Note:** Fold and pin free edges of appliqués away from seam allowances. After assembling the quilt top, fuse, then blanket stitch free edges in place. **Note:** Crystal "eyes" are added to bees after quilting project.

Pear Blossom Block

15

JUNE: Wild Roses

Finished Block Size: 16" x 22" (41 cm x 56 cm)

Fabric Requirements

Yardage is based on 43"/44" (109 cm/112 cm) wide fabric with a usable width of 40" (102 cm).

- 12¹/₂" x 20¹/₂"(32 cm x 53 cm) rectangle of blue batik for **background**
- ¹/₈ yd (11 cm) *each* of 1 cream and 1 black batik for checkerboard border
- 8" x 13" (20 cm x 33 cm) rectangle of white print for fence
- 7" x 8" (18 cm x 20 cm) rectangle of hot pink batik for heart
- 6" x 7" (15 cm x 18 cm) rectangle of black/green batik for wings
- 5" x 8" (13 cm x 20 cm) rectangle of green batik for leaves
- Scraps of purple, hot pink, cream, and green batiks for remaining appliqués

You will also need:

- 1 pair of 3 mm hot-fix crystals for eyes
- Paper-backed fusible web

Cutting the Pieces

*Follow **Rotary Cutting**, page 76, to cut fabric. Cut all strips from the selvage-to-selvage width of the fabric. All measurements include ¹/₄" seam allowances.*

From cream batik:
- Cut 1 **strip** 2¹/₂" wide.

From black batik:
- Cut 1 **strip** 2¹/₂" wide.

Cutting the Appliqués

*Follow **Fusible Appliqué**, page 79, to make appliqués from June patterns, pages 47-48.*

From white print:
- Cut 3 **fence posts** 1¹/₄" x 5³/₄".
- Cut 2 **fence rails** 1¹/₄" x 11".

From hot pink batik:
- Cut 1 **heart**.

From black/green batik:
- Cut 1 **wing**.

From green batik:
- Cut 1 **leaf**. Cut 1 **leaf reversed**.

From scraps of purple, hot pink, cream, and green batiks:
- Cut 15 **petals**.
- Cut 3 **scalloped centers**.
- Cut 1 **body**.
- Cut 3 **oval centers**.
- Cut 2 **stems** ¹/₂" x 8".

Making the Block

*Follow **Piecing** and **Pressing**, page 77. Match right sides and use a ¹/₄" seam allowance.*

1. Referring to **Making Strip Sets**, page 77, use cream and black **strips** to make 1 **Strip Set**. From this, cut 14 **Unit 1's**.

Unit 1 (make 14)

2. Matching short edges, sew 5 Unit 1's together to make **Unit 2**. Make 2 Unit 2's.

Unit 2 (make 2)

3. Matching short edges, sew 4 Unit 1's together to make **Unit 3**.

Unit 3

4. Sew 1 Unit 2 to each long edge of **background** to make **Unit 4**.

Unit 4

5. Sew Unit 3 to Unit 4 to make **Unit 5**.

Unit 5

Adding the Appliqués

*Refer to **Blanket Stitch Appliqué**, page 79, for stitching techniques.*

1. Working from the background up, arrange **appliqués** on Unit 5; fuse.
2. Blanket Stitch around appliqués to complete **Wild Roses** block. **Note:** Crystal "eyes" are added to butterfly after quilting project.

Wild Roses Block

17

JULY: Bounty Of Sunflowers

Finished Block Size: 28" x 12" (71 cm x 30 cm)

Fabric Requirements

Yardage is based on 43"/44" (109 cm/112 cm) wide fabric with a usable width of 40" (102 cm).

26¹/₂" x 8¹/₂"(68 cm x 22 cm) rectangle of grey batik for **background**

¹/₈ yd (11 cm) *each* of 1 cream and 1 black batik for checkerboard border

9" x 21" (23 cm x 53 cm) rectangle of orange batik for flowers

5" x 15" (13 cm x 38 cm) rectangle of cream batik for large centers

4" x 12" (10 cm x 30 cm) rectangle of brown batik for small centers

7" x 8" (18 cm x 20 cm) rectangle of purple batik for basket

5" x 10" (13 cm x 25 cm) rectangle of violet batik for berries

17" x 17" (43 cm x 43 cm) square of green batik for stems

You will also need:

¹/₂" (12 mm) wide bias tape maker

Fabric basting glue

Paper-backed fusible web

Cutting the Pieces

*Follow **Rotary Cutting**, page 76, to cut fabric. Cut all strips from the selvage-to-selvage width of the fabric. All measurements include ¹/₄" seam allowances.*

From cream batik:
- Cut 1 **strip** 2¹/₂" wide.

From black batik:
- Cut 1 **strip** 2¹/₂" wide.

Cutting the Appliqués

*Follow **Fusible Appliqué**, page 79, to make appliqués from July patterns, pages 48-49.*

From orange batik:
- Cut 3 **flowers**.

From cream batik:
- Cut 3 **large flower centers**.

From brown batik:
- Cut 3 **small flower centers**.

From purple batik:
- Cut 1 **basket**.
- Cut 1 **basket handle**.

From violet batik:
- Cut 8 **berries**.

From green batik:
- Cut 1 **bias strip** 1" x 22".
- Cut 3 **bias strips** 1" x 6".

Making the Block

Follow *Piecing* and *Pressing*, page 77. Match right sides and use a ¹/₄" seam allowance.

1. Referring to **Making Strip Sets**, page 77, use cream and black **strips** to make 1 **Strip Set**. From this, cut 16 Unit 1's.

Unit 1 (make 16)

2. Matching short edges, sew 2 Unit 1's together to make Unit 2.

Unit 2

3. Matching long edges, sew 14 Unit 1's together to make Unit 3.

Unit 3

4. Sew Unit 2 to **background** to make Unit 4.

Unit 4

5. Sew Unit 3 to Unit 4 to make Unit 5.

Unit 5

Adding the Appliqués

*Refer to **Blanket Stitch Appliqué**, page 79, for stitching techniques.*

1. Using the bias tape maker, follow the manufacturer's instructions to make ¹/₂" wide **stems** from **bias strips**.
2. Trimming as needed, arrange stems on Unit 5; secure with drops of basting glue. Blanket Stitch stems in place.
3. Working from the background up, arrange remaining **appliqués** on Unit 5; fuse.
4. Blanket Stitch around appliqués to complete Bounty Of Sunflowers Block.

Bounty Of Sunflowers Block

AUGUST: Delightful Pinks

Finished Block Size: 12" x 28" (30 cm x 71 cm)

Fabric Requirements

Yardage is based on 43"/44" (109 cm/112 cm) wide fabric with a usable width of 40" (102 cm).

 8¹/₂" x 22¹/₂" (22 cm x 57 cm) rectangle of tan batik for **background**

 ¹/₄ yd (23 cm) *each* of 1 cream and 1 black batik for checkerboard border

 9" x 11" (23 cm x 28 cm) rectangle of violet batik for basket

 5" x 5" (13 cm x 13 cm) square of gold batik for stars

 4" x 8" (10 cm x 20 cm) rectangle of black/green batik for calyxes

 3" x 11" (8 cm x 28 cm) rectangle of green batik for stems

 Scraps of hot pink, purple, cream, gold, and black batiks for remaining appliqués

You will also need:

 1 pair of 3 mm hot-fix crystals for eyes
 Paper-backed fusible web

Cutting the Pieces

*Follow **Rotary Cutting**, page 76, to cut fabric. Cut all strips from the selvage-to-selvage width of the fabric. All measurements include ¹/₄" seam allowances.*

From cream batik:
- Cut 2 **strips** 2¹/₂" wide.

From black batik:
- Cut 2 **strips** 2¹/₂" wide.

Cutting the Appliqués

*Follow **Fusible Appliqué**, page 77, to make appliqués from August patterns, pages 49-50.*

From violet batik:
- Cut 1 **basket**.
- Cut 1 **basket handle**.

From gold batik:
- Cut 3 **stars**.

From black/green batik:
- Cut 3 **calyxes**.

From green batik:
- Cut 1 **long stem** ¹/₂" x 10".
- Cut 1 **medium stem** ¹/₂" x 6".
- Cut 1 **short stem** ¹/₂" x 4".

From scraps of hot pink, purple , cream, gold, and black batiks:
- Cut a *total* of 12 **petals**.
- Cut 1 **bee**.
- Cut 1 **wing**.
- Cut 1 of each **stripe A-B**.

Making the Block

*Follow **Piecing** and **Pressing**, page 77. Match right sides and use a ¹/₄" seam allowance.*

1. Referring to **Making Strip Sets**, page 77, use cream and black **strips** to make 2 **Strip Sets**. From these, cut 20 Unit 1's.

Unit 1 (make 20)

2. Matching short edges, sew 2 Unit 1's together to make Unit 2.

Unit 2

3. Matching long edges, sew 4 Unit 1's together to make Unit 3.

Unit 3

4. Matching short edges, sew 7 Unit 1's together to make Unit 4. Make 2 Unit 4's.

Unit 4 (make 2)

5. Sew Unit 2 and Unit 3 to **background** to make Unit 5.

Unit 5

6. Sew Unit 4's to Unit 5 to make Unit 6.

Unit 6

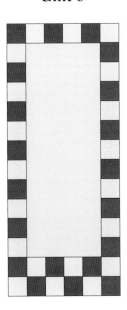

Adding the Appliqués

*Refer to **Blanket Stitch Appliqué**, page 79, for stitching techniques.*

1. Working from the background up and trimming **stems** as needed, arrange **appliqués** on Unit 6; fuse.

2. Blanket Stitch around appliqués to complete Delightful Pinks block. **Note:** Crystal "eyes" are added to bee after quilting project.

Delightful Pinks Block

SEPTEMBER: Once in a Blue Moon

Finished Block Size: 8" x 28" (20 cm x 71 cm)

Fabric Requirements

Yardage is based on 43"/44" (109 cm/112 cm) wide fabric with a usable width of 40" (102 cm).

- 8¹/₂" x 22¹/₂" (22 cm x 58 cm) rectangle of brown batik for **background**
- ¹/₈ yd (11 cm) *each* of 1 cream and 1 black batik for checkerboard border
- 6" x 6" (15 cm x 15 cm) square of off-white batik for moon
- 5" x 5" (13 cm x 13 cm) square of gold batik for stars
- 5" x 10" (13 cm x 25 cm) rectangle of white print for flowers
- 7" x 10" (18 cm x 25 cm) rectangle of green batik for stems, calyxes, and leaves

You will also need:
- Paper-backed fusible web

Cutting the Pieces

*Follow **Rotary Cutting**, page 76, to cut fabric. Cut all strips from the selvage-to-selvage width of the fabric. All measurements include ¹/₄" seam allowances.*

From cream batik:
- Cut 1 **strip** 2¹/₂" wide.

From black batik:
- Cut 1 **strip** 2¹/₂" wide.

Cutting the Appliqués

*Follow **Fusible Appliqué**, page 79, to make appliqués from September patterns, pages 50-51.*

From off-white batik:
- Cut 1 **moon**.

From gold batik:
- Cut 3 **stars**.

From white print:
- Cut 3 **flowers**.

From green batik:
- Cut 1 **stem**.
- Cut 3 **calyxes**.
- Cut 2 **leaves**.

Making the Block

*Follow **Piecing** and **Pressing**, page 77. Match right sides and use a ¹/₄" seam allowance.*

1. Referring to **Making Strip Sets**, page 77, use cream and black **strips** to make 1 **Strip Set**. From this, cut 6 **Unit 1's**.

Unit 1 (make 6)

2. Matching short edges, sew 2 Unit 1's together to make Unit 2. Make 3 Unit 2's.

Unit 2 (make 3)

3. Matching long edges, sew 3 Unit 2's together to make Unit 3.

Unit 3

4. Sew Unit 3 to **background** to make Unit 4.

Unit 4

Adding the Appliqués

*Refer to **Blanket Stitch Appliqué**, page 79, for stitching techniques.*

1. Working from the background up and trimming **stems** as needed, arrange **appliqués** on Unit 4; fuse. **Note:** For appliqués that extend into the borders of adjacent blocks, leave protruding edges free.
2. Blanket Stitch around appliqués to complete Once In A Blue Moon Block. **Note:** Fold and pin free edges of appliqués away from seam allowances. After assembling the quilt top, fuse, then blanket stitch free edges in place.

Once In A Blue Moon Block

23

OCTOBER:
Candy Corn Toss

Finished Block Size: 14" x 22" (36 cm x 56 cm)

Fabric Requirements

Yardage is based on 43"/44" (109 cm/112 cm) wide fabric with a usable width of 40" (102 cm).

> 10¹/₂" x 16¹/₂" (27 cm x 42 cm) rectangle of grey batik for **background**
>
> ¹/₄ yd (23 cm) *each* of 1 cream and 1 black batik for checkerboard border
>
> 8" x 8" (20 cm x 20 cm) square of blue batik for basket
>
> 10" x 10" (25 cm x 25 cm) square of white print for candy corn
>
> 4" x 7" (10 cm x 18 cm) rectangle of yellow batik for candy corn
>
> 5" x 8" (13 cm x 20 cm) rectangle of orange batik for candy corn
>
> 4" x 8" (10 cm x 20 cm) rectangle of hot pink batik for stars
>
> 8" x 10" (20 cm x 25 cm) rectangle of green batik for stems and leaves

You will also need:

> Paper-backed fusible web

Cutting the Pieces

*Follow **Rotary Cutting**, page 76, to cut fabric. Cut all strips from the selvage-to-selvage width of the fabric. All measurements include ¹/₄" seam allowances.*

From cream batik:
- Cut 2 **strips** 2¹/₂" wide.

From black batik:
- Cut 2 **strips** 2¹/₂" wide.

Cutting the Appliqués

*Follow **Fusible Appliqué**, page 79, to make appliqués from October patterns, pages 51-52.*

From blue batik:
- Cut 1 **basket**.
- Cut 1 **basket handle**.

From white print:
- Cut 4 **candy corn bases**.

From yellow batik:
- Cut 4 **middle candy corn sections**.

From orange batik:
- Cut 4 **lower candy corn sections**.

From hot pink batik:
- Cut 3 **stars**.

From green batik:
- Cut 4 **stems** ¹/₂" x 8".
- Cut 4 **leaves**. Cut 4 **leaves reversed**.

Making the Block
*Follow **Piecing** and **Pressing**, page 77. Match right sides and use a ¹/₄" seam allowance.*

1. Referring to **Making Strip Sets**, page 77, use cream and black **strips** to make 2 **Strip Sets**. From these, cut 19 Unit 1's.

Unit 1 (make 19)

2. Matching short edges, sew 4 Unit 1's together to make Unit 2. Make 2 Unit 2's.

Unit 2 (make 2)

3. Matching short edges, sew 4 Unit 1's together to make Unit 3. Remove 1 black square from 1 end of Unit 3; 7 squares remaining (Fig. 1).

Unit 3

Fig. 1

4. Matching long edges, sew 7 Unit 1's together to make Unit 4.

Unit 4

5. Sew 1 Unit 2 to each long edge of **background** to make Unit 5.

Unit 5

6. Sew Unit 3, then Unit 4 to remaining edges of **Unit 5** to make Unit 6.

Unit 6

Adding the Appliqués

*Refer to **Blanket Stitch Appliqué**, page 79, for stitching techniques.*

1. Working from the background up and trimming **stems** as needed, arrange **appliqués** on Unit 6; fuse.
2. Blanket Stitch around appliqués to complete Candy Corn Toss Block.

Candy Corn Toss Block

NOVEMBER:
Pumpkin Harvest

Finished Block Size: 10" x 22" (25 cm x 56 cm)

Fabric Requirements

Yardage is based on 43"/44" (109 cm/112 cm) wide fabric with a usable width of 40" (102 cm).

- $10^1/_2$" x $12^1/_2$" (27 cm x 32 cm) **large rectangle** of cream batik for background
- $10^1/_2$" x $4^1/_2$" (27 cm x 11 cm) **small rectangle** of green batik #1 for background
- $^1/_8$ yd (11 cm) *each* of 1 cream and 1 black batik for checkerboard border
- 6" x 8" (15 cm x 20 cm) rectangle of green batik #2 for leaves
- 1" x 20" (3 cm x 51 cm) **bias strip** of green batik #3 for stem
- 9" x 12" (23 cm x 30 cm) rectangle of orange batik for pumpkin
- 6" x 6" (15 cm x 15 cm) square of pink batik for flower
- 3" x 3" (8 cm x 8 cm) square of black/green batik flower center
- 3" x 3" (8 cm x 8 cm) rectangle of black batik for pumpkin stem

You will also need:
- $^1/_2$" (12 mm) wide bias tape maker
- Fabric basting glue
- Paper-backed fusible web

Cutting the Pieces

*Follow **Rotary Cutting**, page 76, to cut fabric. Cut all strips from the selvage-to-selvage width of the fabric. All measurements include $^1/_4$" seam allowances.*

From cream batik:
- Cut 1 **strip** $2^1/_2$" wide.

From black batik:
- Cut 1 **strip** $2^1/_2$" wide.

Cutting the Appliqués

*Follow **Fusible Appliqué**, page 77, to make appliqués from November patterns, pages 52-53.*

From green batik #2:
- Cut 8 **leaves**.

From orange batik:
- Cut 1 **pumpkin**.

From pink batik:
- Cut 1 **flower**.

From black/green batik:
- Cut 1 **flower center**.

From black batik:
- Cut 1 **pumpkin stem**.

Making the Block

*Follow **Piecing** and **Pressing**, page 77. Match right sides and use a ¹/₄" seam allowance.*

1. Sew **large** and **small rectangles** together to make background.

Background

2. Referring to **Making Strip Sets**, page 77, use cream and black **strips** to make 1 **Strip Set**. From this, cut 8 Unit 1's.

Unit 1 (make 8)

3. Matching short edges, sew 3 Unit 1's together to make Unit 2. Remove 1 cream square from 1 end of Unit 2; 5 squares remaining (Fig. 1).

Unit 2

Fig. 1

4. Matching long edges, sew 5 Unit 1's together to make Unit 3.

Unit 3

5. Sew Unit 2 to **background** to make Unit 4.

Unit 4

6. Sew Unit 3 to **Unit 4** to make Unit 5.

Unit 5

Adding the Appliqués

*Refer to **Blanket Stitch Appliqué**, page 79, for stitching techniques.*

1. Using the bias tape maker, follow the manufacturer's instructions to make a $^1/_2$" wide **stem** from **bias strip**.

2. Arrange stem on Unit 5; secure with drops of basting glue. Blanket Stitch stem in place.

3. Working from the background up, arrange remaining **appliqués** on Unit 5; fuse. **Note:** For appliqués that extend into the borders of adjacent blocks, leave protruding edges free.

4. Blanket Stitch around appliqués to complete Pumpkin Harvest Block. **Note:** Fold and pin free edges of appliqués away from seam allowances. After assembling the quilt top, fuse, then blanket stitch free edges in place.

Pumpkin Harvest Block

DECEMBER:
Tidings of Joy

Finished Block Size: 20" x 22" (51 cm x 56 cm)

Fabric Requirements

Yardage is based on 43"/44" (109 cm/112 cm) wide fabric with a usable width of 40" (102 cm).

Two $8^1/_2$" x $8^1/_2$" (22 cm x 22 cm) **squares** of grey batik for background

Two $8^1/_2$" x $8^1/_2$" (22 cm x 22 cm) **squares** of blue batik for background

$^1/_4$ yd (23 cm) *each* of 1 cream and 1 black batik for checkerboard border

12" x 15" (30 cm x 38 cm) rectangle of dark green batik for large leaves

1" x 16" (3 cm x 41 cm) **bias strip** of light green batik for stem

10" x 12" (25 cm x 30 cm) rectangle of light green batik for small leaves

11" x 8" (28 cm x 20 cm) rectangle of blue batik for dress

13" x 4" (33 cm x 10 cm) rectangle of purple batik for wings

Scraps of red, gold, peach, and black batiks for remaining appliqués

You will also need:

1 pair of 3 mm hot-fix crystals for eyes

$^1/_2$" (12 mm) wide bias tape maker

Fabric basting glue

Paper-backed fusible web

Cutting the Pieces

*Follow **Rotary Cutting**, page 76, to cut fabric. Cut all strips from the selvage-to-selvage width of the fabric. All measurements include ¹/₄" seam allowances.*

From cream batik:
- Cut 2 **strips** 2¹/₂" wide.

From black batik:
- Cut 2 **strips** 2¹/₂" wide.

Cutting the Appliqués

*Follow **Fusible Appliqué**, page 79, to make appliqués from December patterns, pages 53-55.*

From dark green batik:
- Cut 6 **large leaves**.

From light green batik:
- Cut 6 **small leaves**.

From blue batik:
- Cut 1 **dress**.
- Cut 1 **sleeve**. Cut 1 **sleeve reversed**.

From purple batik:
- Cut 1 **wing**.

From scraps of red, gold, peach, and black batiks:
- Cut 2 **berries**.
- Cut 2 **stars**.
- Cut 1 **face**.
- Cut 1 **halo**.
- Cut 1 **hair**.

Making the Block

*Follow **Piecing** and **Pressing**, page 77. Match right sides and use a ¹/₄" seam allowance.*

1. Sew blue and grey **squares** together to make **background**.

Background

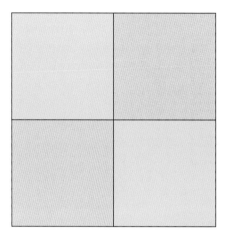

2. Referring to **Making Strip Sets**, page 77, use cream and black **strips** to make 2 **Strip Sets**. From these, cut 23 **Unit 1's**.

Unit 1 (make 23)

3. Matching short edges, sew 4 Unit 1's together to make **Unit 2**. Make 2 Unit 2's.

Unit 2 (make 2)

4. Matching short edges, sew 5 Unit 1's together to make **Unit 3**.

Unit 3

5. Matching long edges, sew 10 Unit 1's together to make **Unit 4**.

Unit 4

6. Sew 1 Unit 2 to opposite edges of **background** to make **Unit 5**.

Unit 5

7. Sew Unit 3, then Unit 4 to remaining edges of **Unit 5** to make **Unit 6**.

Unit 6

Adding the Appliqués

*Refer to **Blanket Stitch Appliqué**, page 79, for stitching techniques.*

1. Using the bias tape maker, follow the manufacturer's instructions to make a $1/2$" wide **stem** from **bias strip**.
2. Arrange stem on Unit 6; secure with drops of basting glue. Blanket Stitch stem in place.
3. Working from the background up, arrange remaining **appliqués** on Unit 6; fuse.
4. Blanket Stitch around appliqués to complete Tidings Of Joy block. **Note:** Crystal "eyes" are added to angel after quilting project.

Tidings Of Joy Block

MAKING THE QUILT
Version I *shown on page 32*

Fabric Requirements

Yardage is based on 43"/44" (109 cm/112 cm) wide fabric with a usable width of 40" (102 cm). Yardage listed below is for inner borders, outer borders, border appliqués, backing, and binding.

- 3 yds (2.7 m) of blue batik for outer border and binding
- $^3/_8$ yd (34 cm) of orange batik for inner border
- $^3/_4$ yd (69 cm) of green batik for border vine
- Scraps of assorted green, orange, gold, pink, and purple batiks for border appliqués
- $7^3/_4$ yds (7 m) of fabric for backing

You will also need:

- 93" x 93" (236 cm x 236 cm) piece of batting
- $^1/_2$" (12 mm) wide bias tape maker
- Fabric basting glue
- Paper-backed fusible web

Cutting the Pieces

*Follow **Rotary Cutting**, page 76, to cut fabric. Cut all strips from the selvage-to-selvage width of the fabric, unless otherwise noted. Border lengths are exact. All measurements include $^1/_4$" seam allowances.*

From blue batik:
- Cut 10 **binding strips** $2^1/_4$" wide.
- Cut 2 *lengthwise* **top/bottom outer borders** $9^1/_2$" x $66^1/_2$".
- Cut 2 *lengthwise* **side outer borders** $9^1/_2$" x $84^1/_2$".

From orange batik:
- Cut 2 **top/bottom inner borders** $1^1/_2$" x $64^1/_2$", piecing as necessary.
- Cut 2 **side inner borders** $1^1/_2$" x $66^1/_2$", piecing as necessary.

From green batik:
- Cut 1 **square** 21" x 21".

Cutting the Appliqués

*Follow **Fusible Appliqué**, page 79, to make appliqués from patterns, page 37.*

From assorted batik scraps:*
- Cut 42 **berries**.
- Cut 64 **petals**.
- Cut 16 **calyxes**.
- Cut 19 **leaves**.

*Includes scraps leftover after cutting inner borders and square for vine

Assembling the Quilt Top Center

*Follow **Piecing** and **Pressing**, page 77. Match right sides and use a $^1/_4$" seam allowance.*

1. Sew **Fun In the Snow**, **Love Blooms**, and **Welcome Home** blocks together to make **Unit 1**.

Unit 1

2. Sew **Delightful Pinks** and **Once In A Blue Moon** blocks together to make **Unit 2**.

Unit 2

Version I

3. Sew **Spring Breeze** block and **Unit 2** together to make Unit 3.

Unit 3

4. Sew **Pear Blossoms** and **Bounty of Sunflowers** blocks together to make Unit 4.

Unit 4

5. Sew **Unit 4** and **Wild Roses** Block together to make Unit 5.

Unit 5

6. Sew **Candy Corn Toss**, **Pumpkin Harvest**, and **Tidings Of Joy** blocks together to make Unit 6.

Unit 6

7. Sew **Units 5** and **6** together to make Unit 7.

Unit 7

8. Sew **Units 3** and **7** together to make Unit 8.

Unit 8

9. Referring to photo, sew **Unit 1** and **Unit 8** together to make quilt top center.

Adding the Borders

1. Matching centers and corners, sew **top/bottom inner borders** to the quilt top center. Repeat to add **side inner borders**.

2. Matching centers and corners, sew **top/bottom outer border** to the quilt top center. Repeat to add **side outer borders**.

Adding the Appliqués

*Refer to **Blanket Stitch Appliqué**, page 79, for stitching techniques.*

1. Referring to **Continuous Bias Strips**, page 82, use **square** to make a 1" wide x 360" long **bias strip**.

2. Using the bias tape maker, follow the manufacturer's instructions to make a $1/2$" wide bias **vine** from bias strip.

3. Arrange vine around outer border; secure with drops of basting glue. Blanket Stitch vine in place.

4. Arrange petals, calyxes, leaves and berries on outer border; fuse. Blanket Stitch around appliqués.

Completing the Quilt

1. Follow **Quilting**, page 80, to mark, layer, and quilt as desired. My quilt is machine quilted with outline quilting around the appliqués. The blocks are quilted with assorted meandering, echo, and swirl designs. The border has an all-over loop and swirl pattern.

2. If desired, follow **Adding A Hanging Sleeve**, page 82, to add a hanging sleeve.

3. Use **binding strips** and follow **Continuous Straight-Grain Strips**, page 84, to make **binding**. Follow **Attaching Binding with Mitered Corners**, page 84, to bind quilt.

4. Follow manufacturer's instructions to add crystal "eyes" to the appliqués.

MAKING THE QUILT
Version II

Fabric Requirements

Yardage is based on 43"/44" (109 cm/112 cm) wide fabric with a usable width of 40" (102 cm). Yardage listed below is for inner borders, outer borders, border appliqués, backing, and binding.

$2^1/8$ yds (1.9 m) of tan print for outer border
$3/8$ yd (34 cm) of brown print for inner border
$3/4$ yd (69 cm) of green print for border vine
$3/8$ yd (34 cm) of red print for corner squares
$7/8$ yd (80 cm) of red stripe for binding
Scraps of assorted green, red, cream, purple, blue, pink, and brown print fabrics for border appliqués
$7^3/4$ yds (7 m) of fabric for backing

You will also need:

93" x 93" (236 cm x 236 cm) piece of batting
$1/2$" (12 mm) wide bias tape maker
Fabric basting glue
Paper-backed fusible web

Cutting the Pieces

*Follow **Rotary Cutting**, page 76, to cut fabric. Cut all strips from the selvage-to-selvage width of the fabric. Border lengths are exact. All measurements include $1/4$" seam allowances.*

From tan print:
- Cut 4 **outer borders** $9^1/2$" x $66^1/2$", piecing as necessary.

From brown print:
- Cut 2 **top/bottom inner borders** $1^1/2$" x $64^1/2$", piecing as necessary.
- Cut 2 **side inner borders** $1^1/2$" x $66^1/2$", piecing as necessary.

From red print:
- Cut 4 **corner squares** $9^1/2$" x $9^1/2$".

From red stripe:
- Cut 1 **binding square** 26" x 26.

Cutting the Appliqués

Follow **Fusible Appliqué**, page 79, to make appliqués from patterns.

From green print:
- Cut 1 **square** 18" x 18".

From assorted print scraps:*
- Cut 18 **berries** (page 37).
- Cut 22 **leaves** (page 37).
- Cut 16 **petals** (page 37).
- Cut 4 **calyxes** (page 37).
- Cut 1 **bird wing reversed** (page 41).
- Cut 1 **bird reversed** (page 42).
- Cut 13 **small stars** (page 42).
- Cut 1 **eye** (page 43).
- Cut 5 **large stars** (page 44).
- Cut 3 **dragonfly bodies** (page 44).
- Cut 3 **large dragonfly wings** (page 44).
- Cut 3 **small dragonfly wings** (page 44).
- Cut 3 **bees** (page 46).
- Cut 3 of *each* **bee stripe** (page 46).
- Cut 3 **bee wings** (page 46).
- Cut 1 **basket** (page 48).
- Cut 1 **basket handle** (page 48).
- Cut 6 **flowers** (page 50).
- Cut 6 **calyxes** (page 50).

*Includes scraps leftover after cutting inner borders and square for vine

Assembling the Quilt Top

1. Follow Steps 1-9 of **Assembling The Quilt Top Center**, page 31, and Step 1 of **Adding The Borders**, page 34.
2. Matching centers and corners, sew 1 **outer border** to opposite sides of quilt top center.
3. Sew 1 **corner square** to each end of remaining 2 outer borders.
4. Sew 1 outer border to each remaining side of quilt top center.

Adding the Appliqués

Refer to **Blanket Stitch Appliqué**, page 79, for stitching techniques.

1. Referring to **Continuous Bias Strips**, page 82, use **square** to make a 1" wide x 270" long **bias strip**.
2. Using the bias tape maker, follow the manufacturer's instructions to make a $1/2$" wide bias **vine** from bias strip.
3. Trimming as needed, arrange vines on outer borders; secure with drops of basting. Blanket Stitch vines in place.
4. Arrange remaining appliqués on outer borders; fuse. Blanket Stitch around appliqués.

Completing the Quilt

1. Follow **Quilting**, page 80, to mark, layer, and quilt as desired. My quilt is machine quilted with outline quilting around the appliqués and loops in the block backgrounds and outer border. There are feather wreaths in the corner squares and an X through the center of each checkerboard square.
2. If desired, follow **Adding A Hanging Sleeve**, page 82, to add a hanging sleeve.
3. Referring to **Continuous Bias Strips**, page 82, use **binding square** to make a $1^1/2$" wide x 360" long **binding strip**.
4. Use **binding strip** and follow **Attaching Binding with Overlapped Corners**, page 86, to bind quilt.
5. Follow manufacturer's instructions to add crystal "eyes" to the appliqués, if desired.

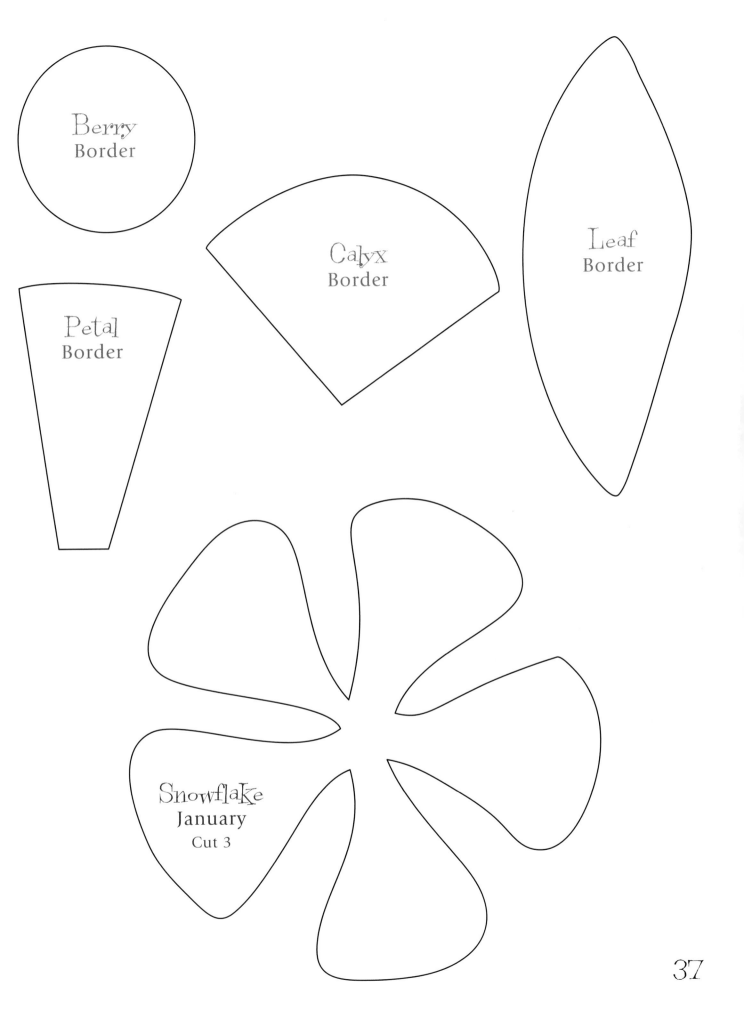

Berry
Border

Calyx
Border

Leaf
Border

Petal
Border

Snowflake
January
Cut 3

37

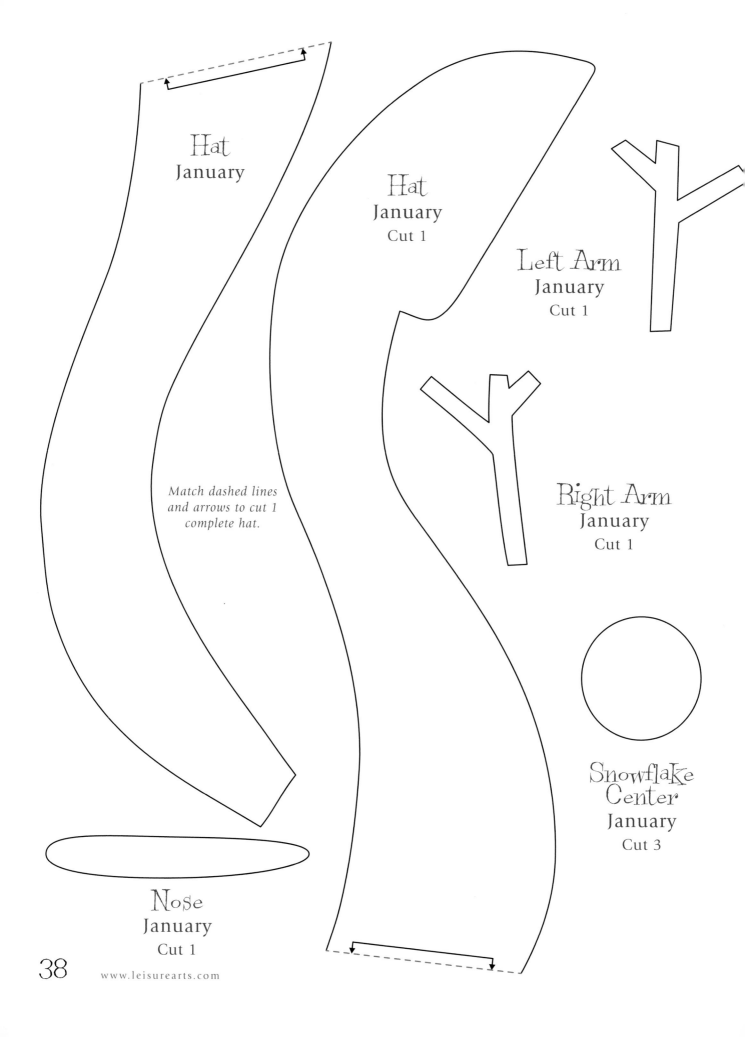

Hat
January

Hat
January
Cut 1

Left Arm
January
Cut 1

Right Arm
January
Cut 1

Match dashed lines
and arrows to cut 1
complete hat.

Snowflake
Center
January
Cut 3

Nose
January
Cut 1

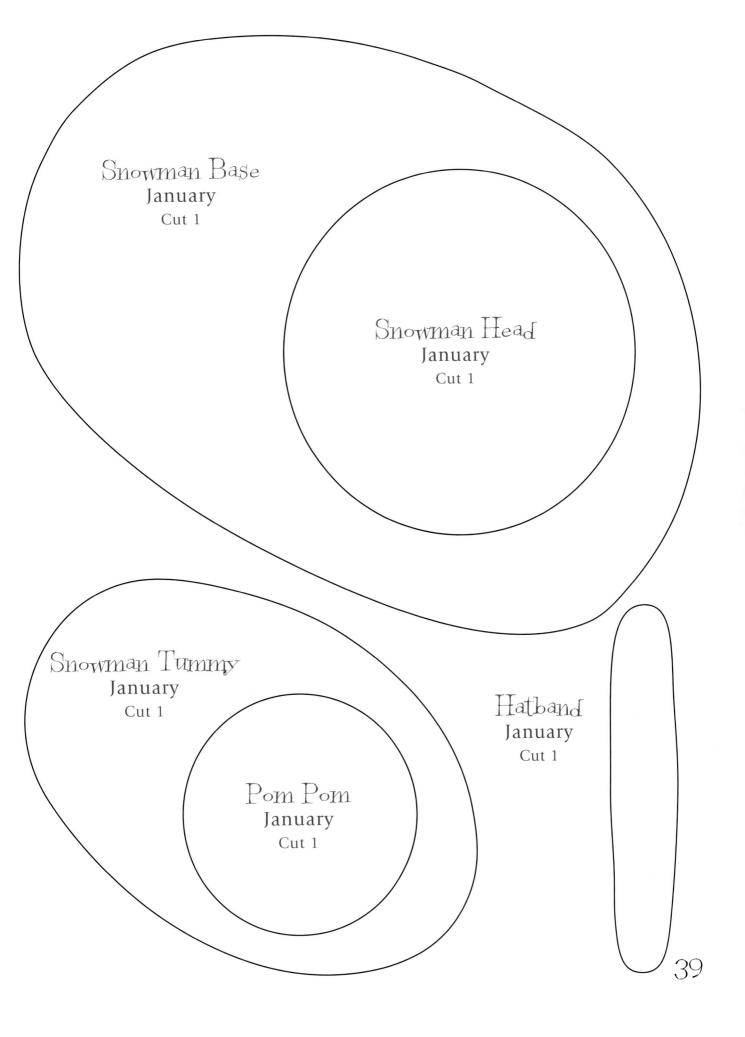

Snowman Base
January
Cut 1

Snowman Head
January
Cut 1

Snowman Tummy
January
Cut 1

Pom Pom
January
Cut 1

Hatband
January
Cut 1

39

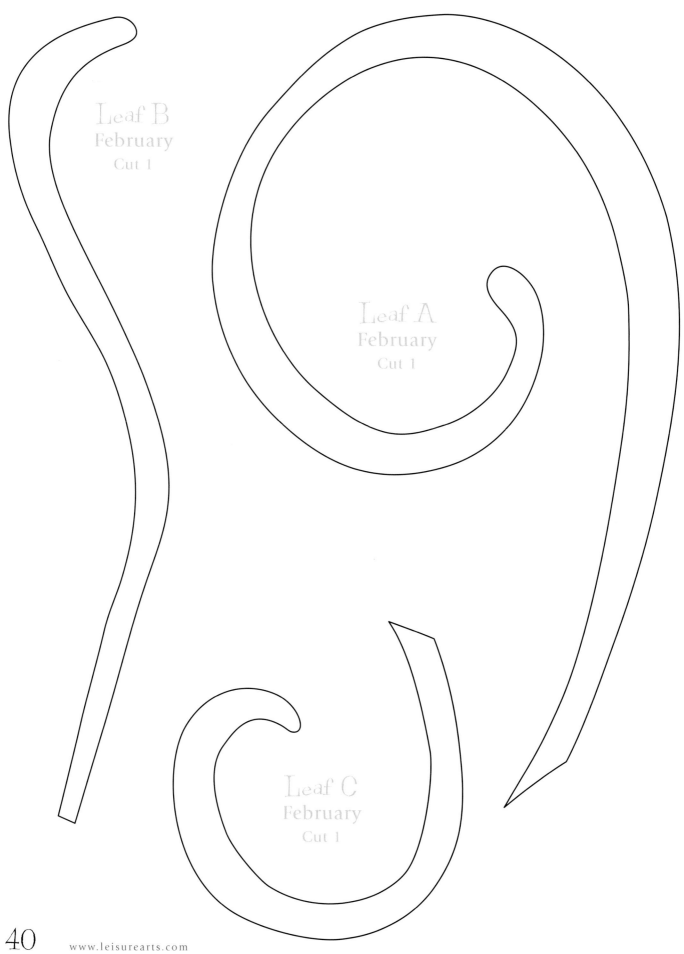

Leaf B
February
Cut 1

Leaf A
February
Cut 1

Leaf C
February
Cut 1

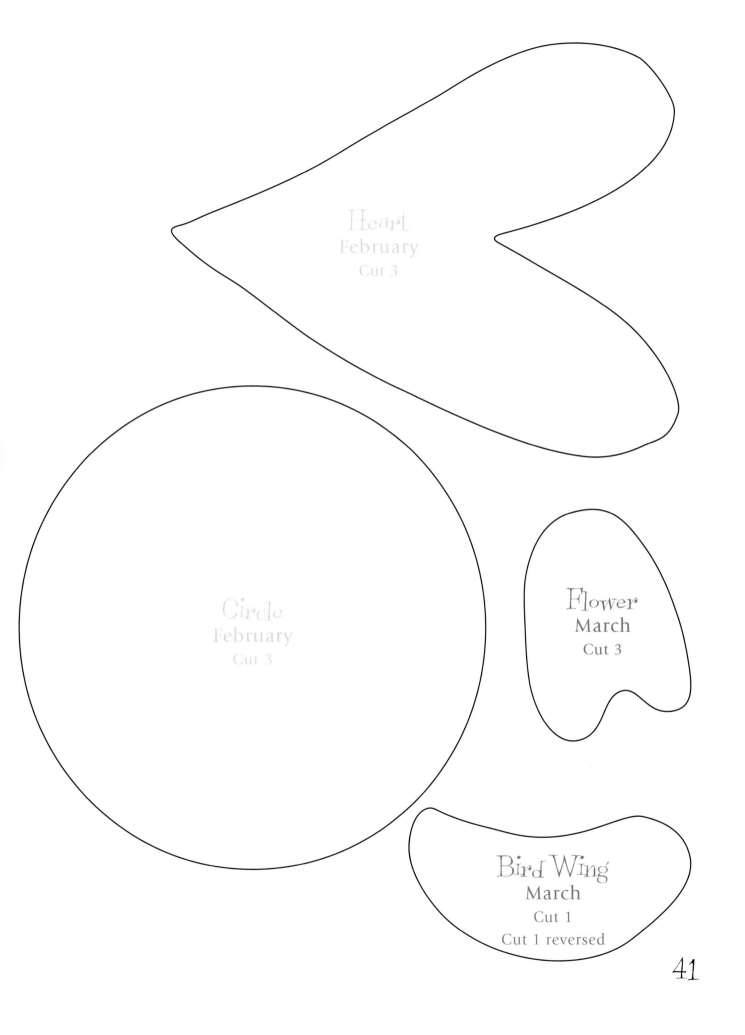

Heart
February
Cut 3

Circle
February
Cut 3

Flower
March
Cut 3

Bird Wing
March
Cut 1
Cut 1 reversed

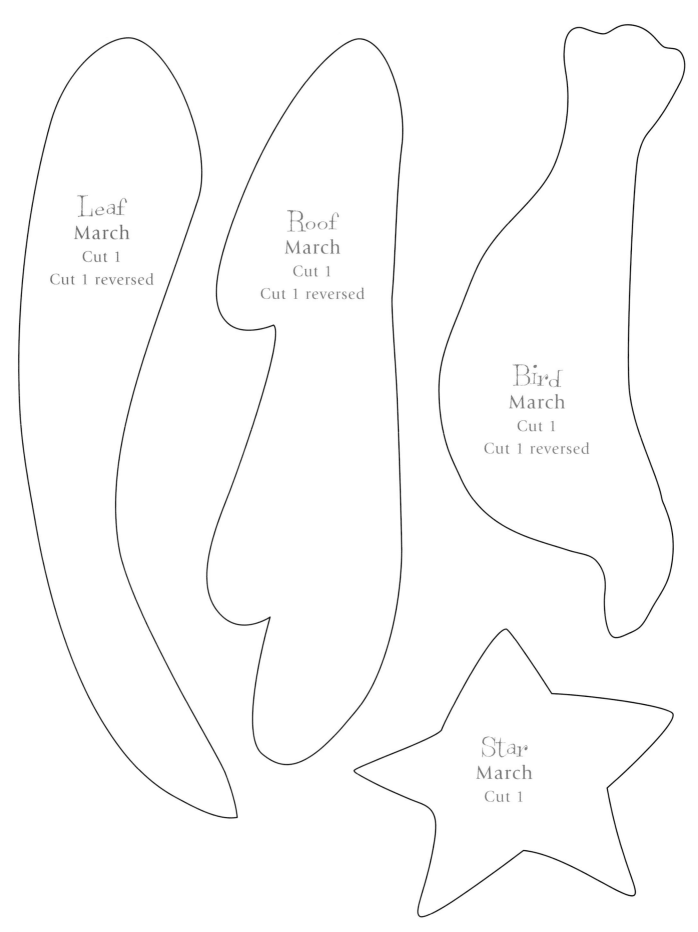

Leaf
March
Cut 1
Cut 1 reversed

Roof
March
Cut 1
Cut 1 reversed

Bird
March
Cut 1
Cut 1 reversed

Star
March
Cut 1

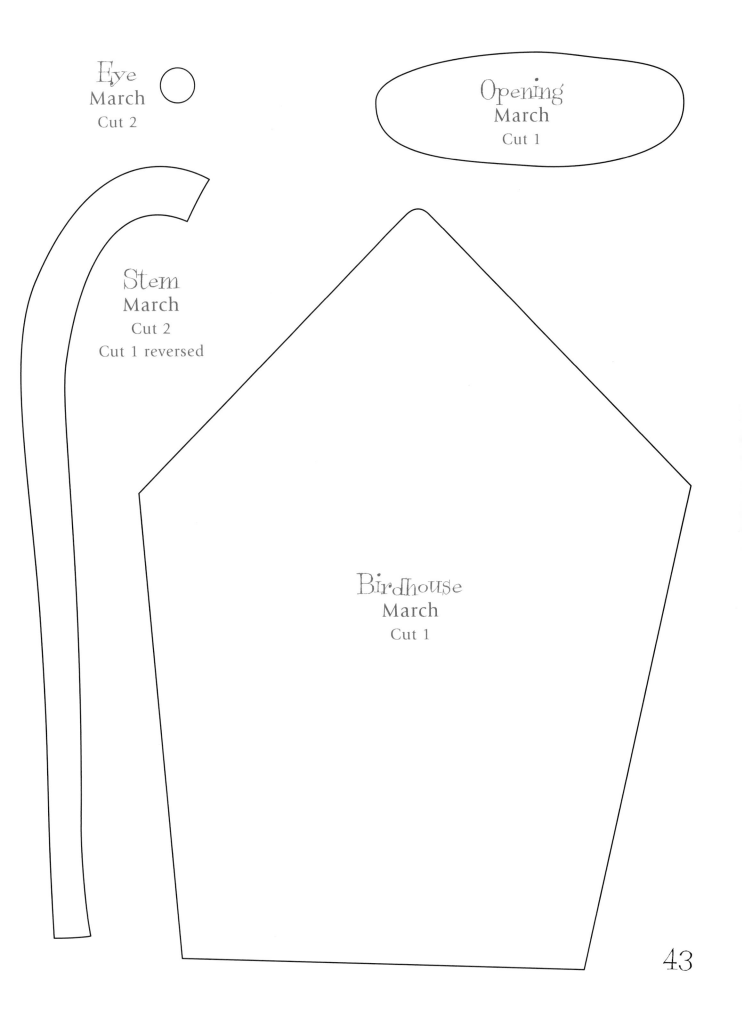

Eye
March
Cut 2

Opening
March
Cut 1

Stem
March
Cut 2
Cut 1 reversed

Birdhouse
March
Cut 1

43

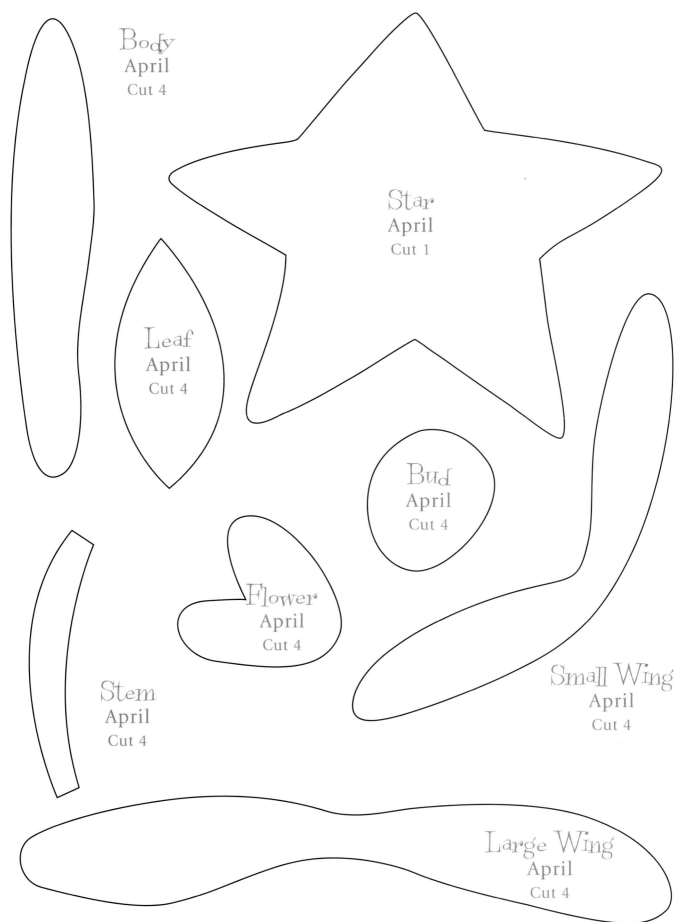

Body
April
Cut 4

Star
April
Cut 1

Leaf
April
Cut 4

Bud
April
Cut 4

Flower
April
Cut 4

Stem
April
Cut 4

Small Wing
April
Cut 4

Large Wing
April
Cut 4

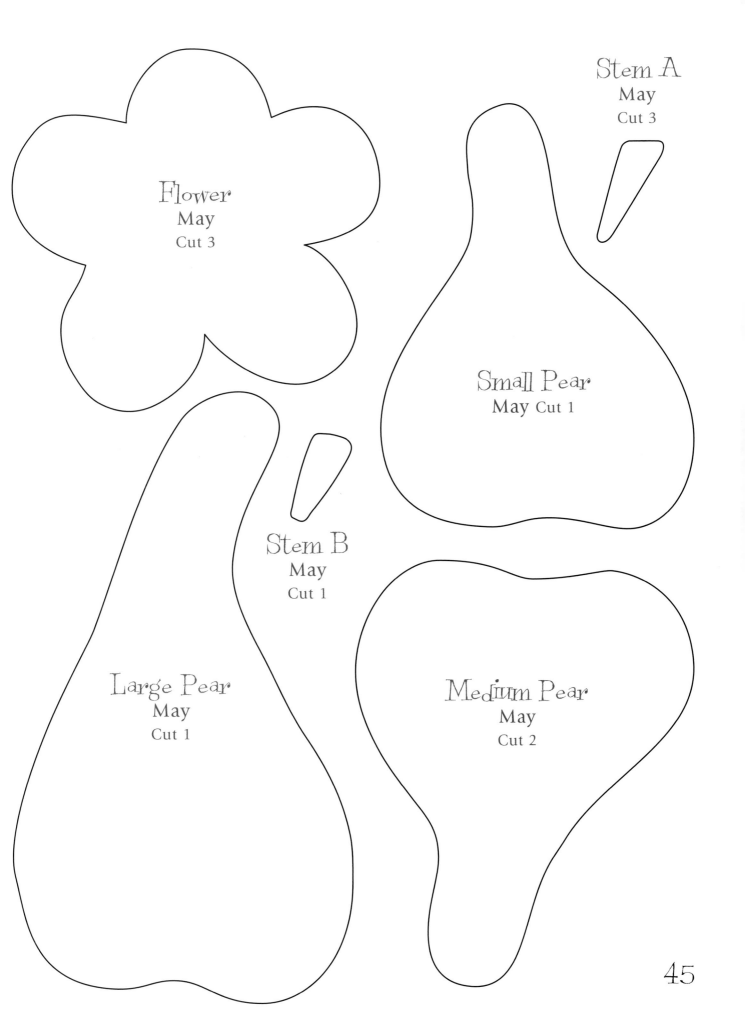

Stem A
May
Cut 3

Flower
May
Cut 3

Small Pear
May Cut 1

Stem B
May
Cut 1

Large Pear
May
Cut 1

Medium Pear
May
Cut 2

45

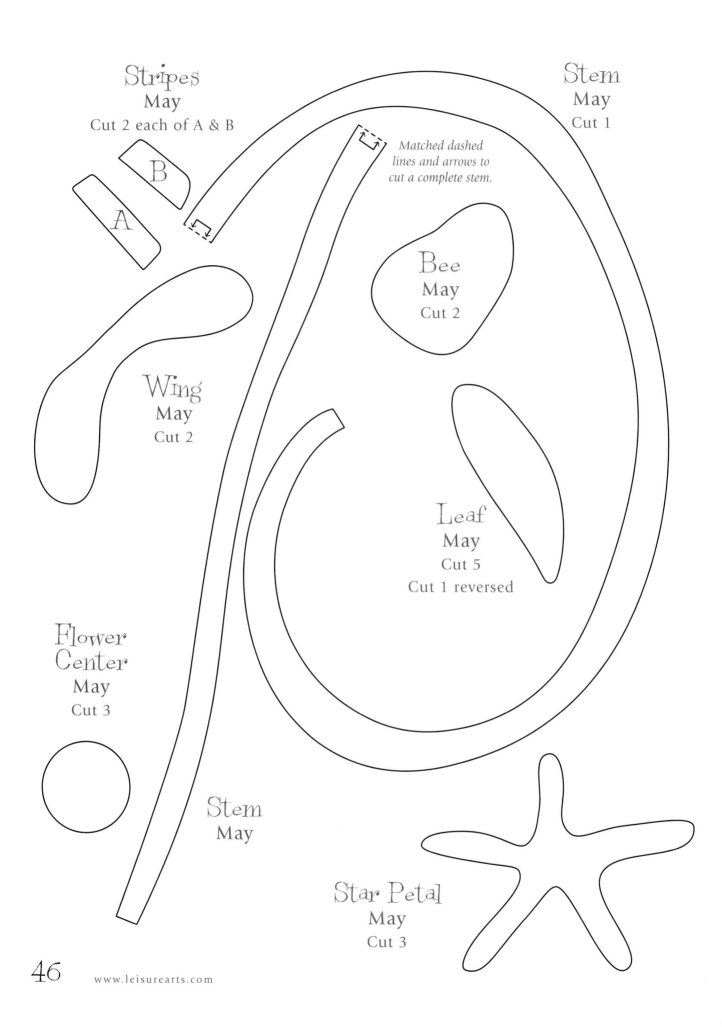

Stripes
May
Cut 2 each of A & B

B

A

Stem
May
Cut 1

Matched dashed lines and arrows to cut a complete stem.

Bee
May
Cut 2

Wing
May
Cut 2

Leaf
May
Cut 5
Cut 1 reversed

Flower Center
May
Cut 3

Stem
May

Star Petal
May
Cut 3

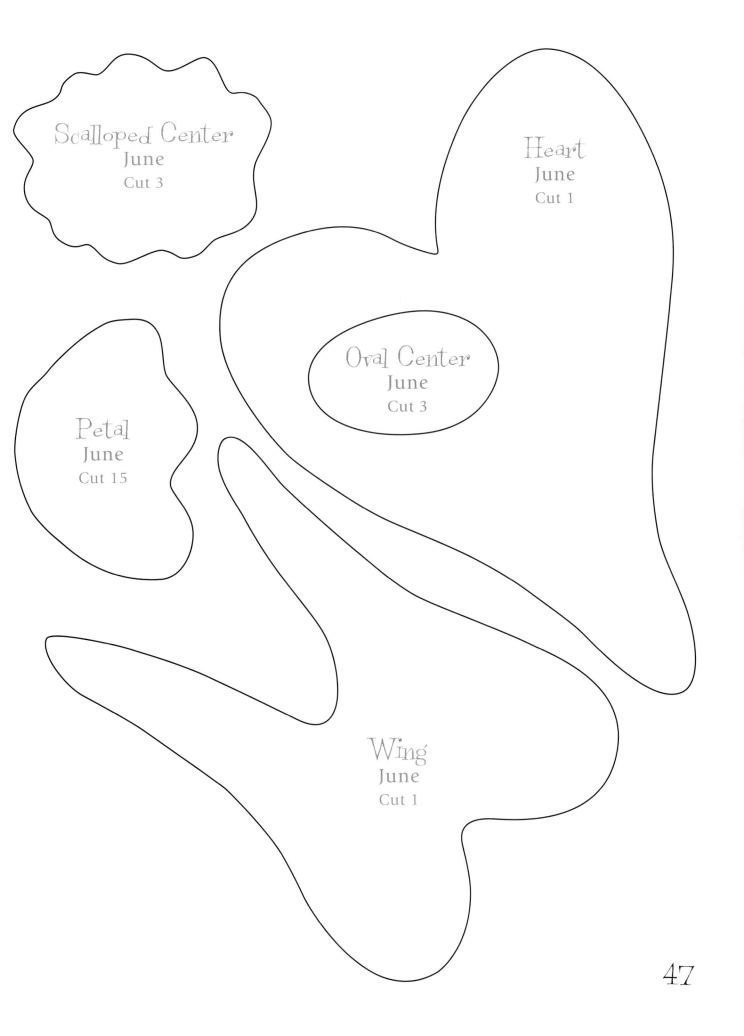

Scalloped Center
June
Cut 3

Heart
June
Cut 1

Petal
June
Cut 15

Oval Center
June
Cut 3

Wing
June
Cut 1

47

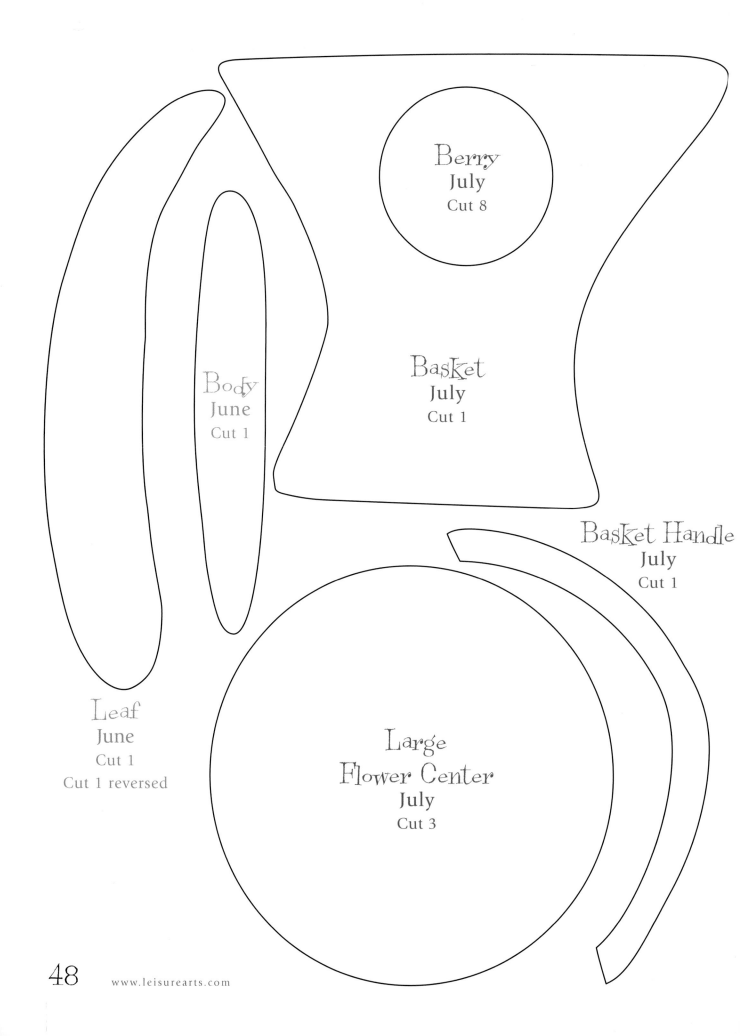

Berry
July
Cut 8

Basket
July
Cut 1

Body
June
Cut 1

Basket Handle
July
Cut 1

Leaf
June
Cut 1
Cut 1 reversed

Large
Flower Center
July
Cut 3

Petal
August
Cut 12

Flower
July
Cut 3

Small
Flower Center
July
Cut 3

Calyx
August
Cut 3

Bee
August
Cut 1

Wing
August
Cut 1

Stripes
August
Cut 1 of each A-B

A

B

Star
August
Cut 3

49

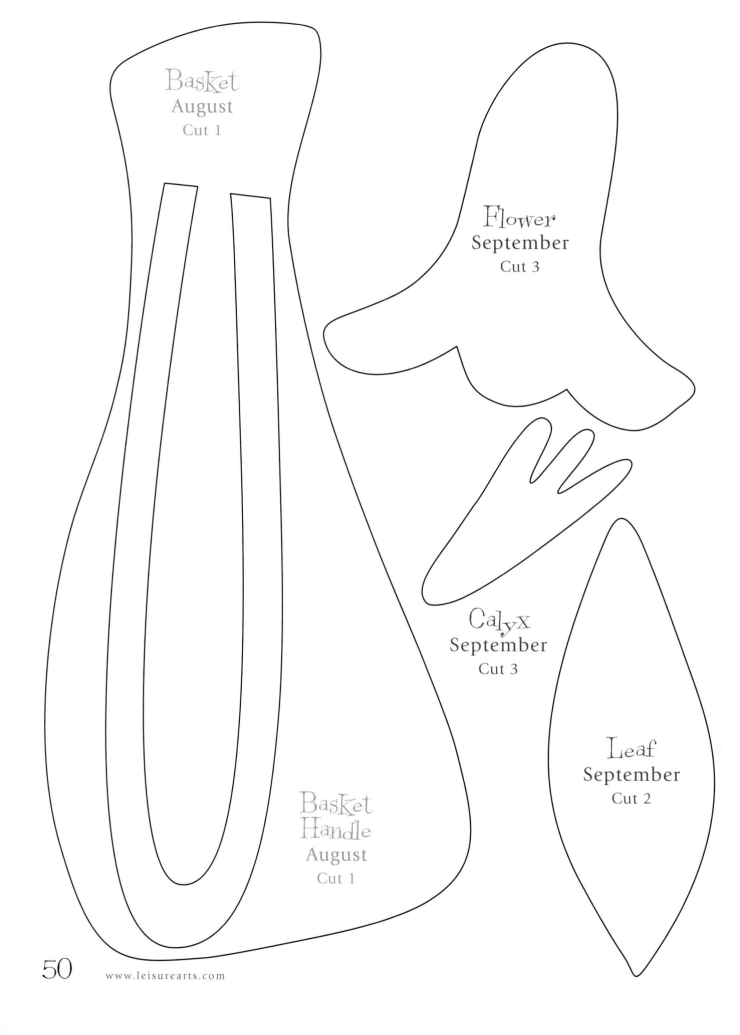

Basket
August
Cut 1

Flower
September
Cut 3

Basket
Handle
August
Cut 1

Calyx
September
Cut 3

Leaf
September
Cut 2

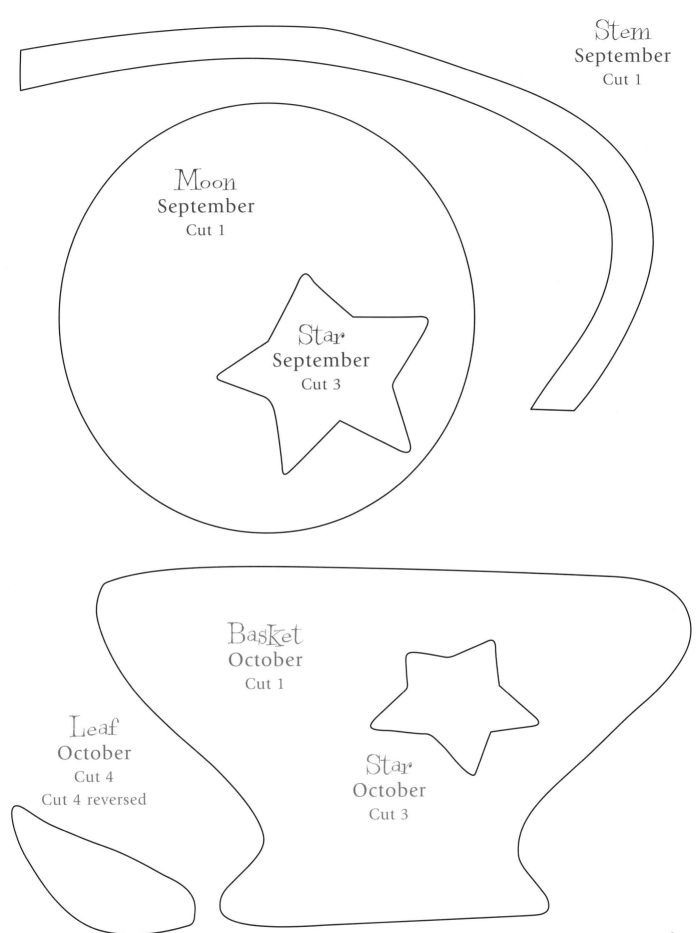

Stem
September
Cut 1

Moon
September
Cut 1

Star
September
Cut 3

Basket
October
Cut 1

Leaf
October
Cut 4
Cut 4 reversed

Star
October
Cut 3

51

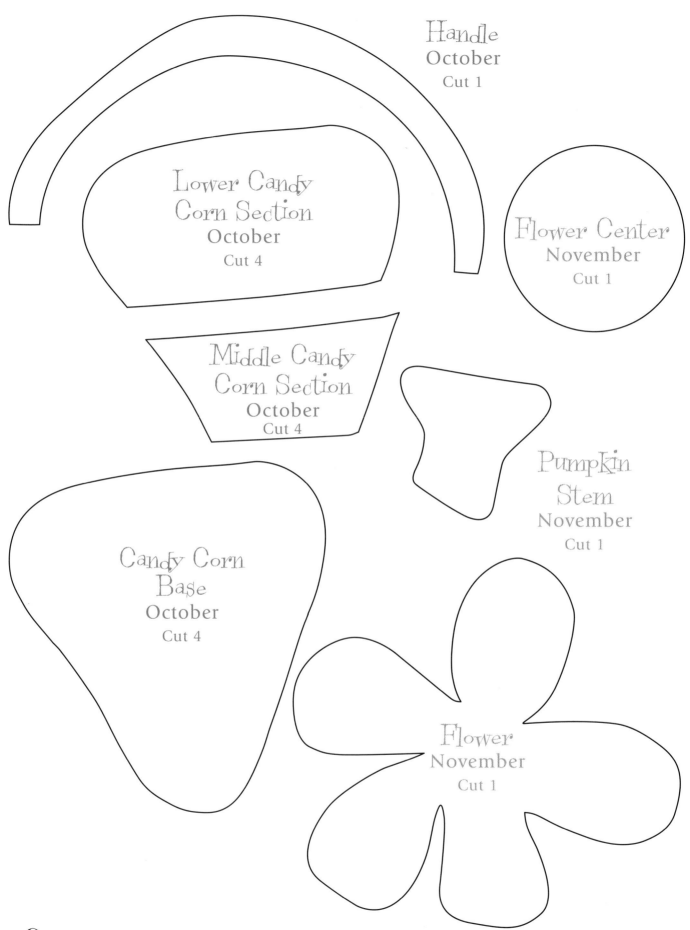

Handle
October
Cut 1

Lower Candy
Corn Section
October
Cut 4

Flower Center
November
Cut 1

Middle Candy
Corn Section
October
Cut 4

Pumpkin
Stem
November
Cut 1

Candy Corn
Base
October
Cut 4

Flower
November
Cut 1

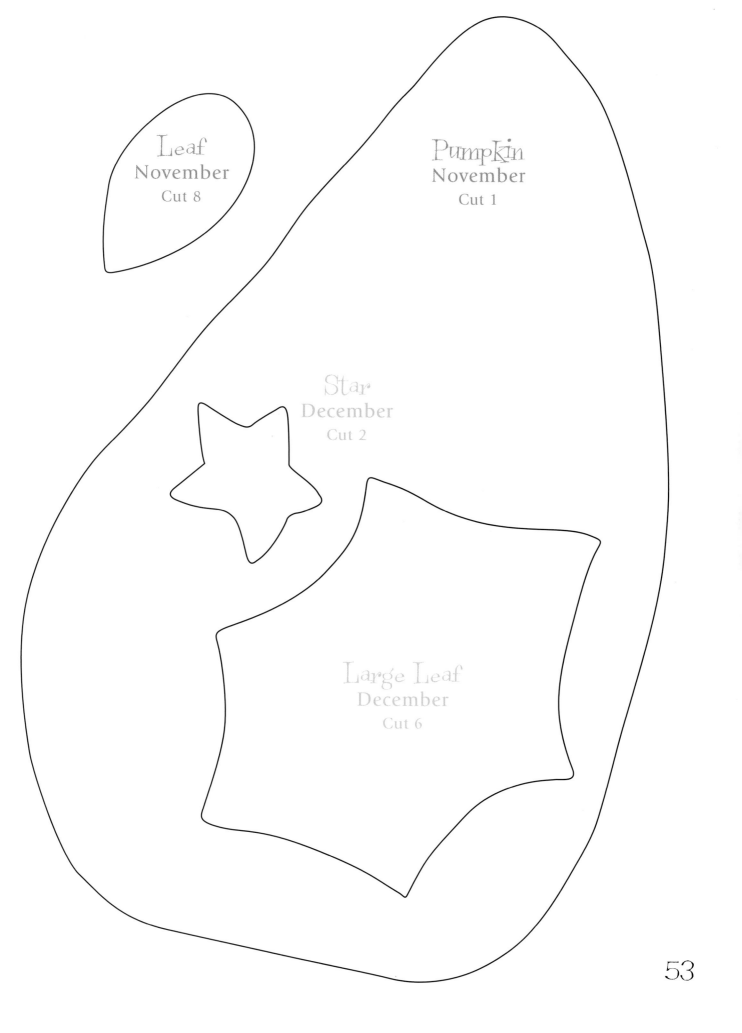

Leaf
November
Cut 8

Pumpkin
November
Cut 1

Star
December
Cut 2

Large Leaf
December
Cut 6

53

Wings
December
Cut 1

Small Leaf
December
Cut 6

Halo
December
Cut 1

Berry
December
Cut 2

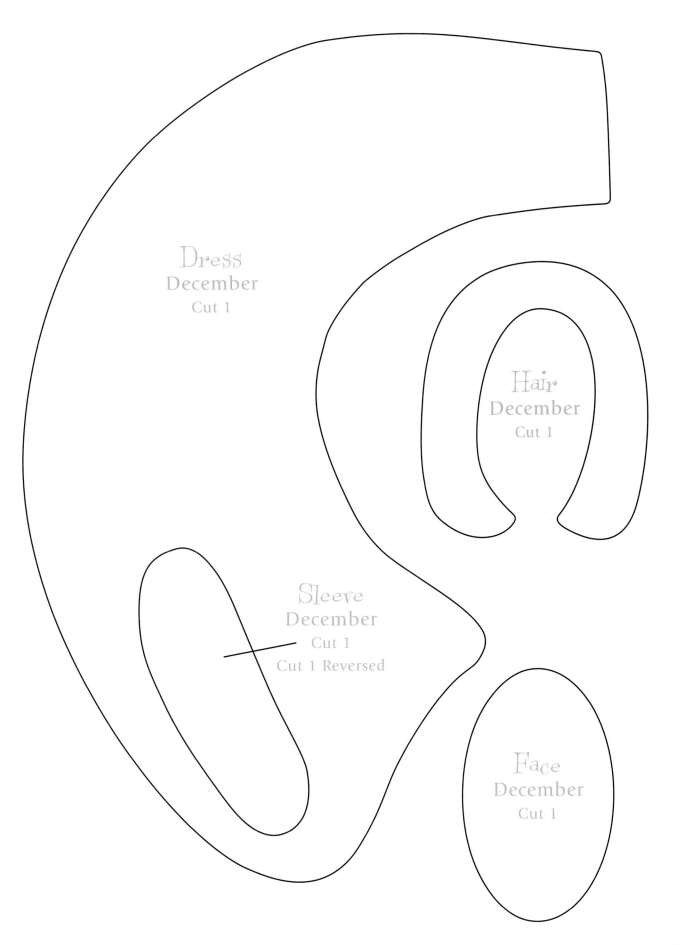

Dress
December
Cut 1

Hair
December
Cut 1

Sleeve
December
Cut 1
Cut 1 Reversed

Face
December
Cut 1

in the pink

I was so inspired by this amazing grey and pink floral fabric that I just had to make a quilt to showcase the beautiful print. This "strippy" design works great for any fabric, but is particularly effective for large scale prints. For the appliqués, I chose the Delightful Pinks flowers from the August block, page 20, and added bias strip stems.

Finished Size: 44" x 57" (112 cm x 145 cm)

Fabric Requirements

Yardage is based on 43"/44" (109 cm/112 cm) wide fabric with a usable width of 40" (102 cm).

- $1^3/_4$ yds (1.6 m) of grey/pink floral print for wide strips
- $1^3/_4$ yds (1.6 m) of cream tone-on-tone print for narrow strips
- $^3/_8$ yd (34 cm) *total* of assorted pink prints for flowers
- $^1/_8$ yd (11 cm) of blue print for berries
- 15" x 15" (38 cm x 38 cm) square of green print for stems
- $^3/_8$ yd (34 cm) *total* of assorted green prints for leaves
- $3^5/_8$ yds (3.3 m) of backing fabric
- $^3/_8$ yd (34 cm) of binding fabric

You will also need:

- 52" x 65" (132 cm x 165 cm) rectangle of batting
- $^1/_2$" (12 mm) wide bias tape maker
- Fabric basting glue
- Paper-backed fusible web

Cutting the Pieces

*Follow **Rotary Cutting**, page 76, to cut fabric. Cut all strips from the selvage-to-selvage width of the fabric unless otherwise noted. All measurements include $^1/_4$" seam allowances.*

From grey/pink print:

- Cut 4 *lengthwise* **wide strips** $7^1/_2$" x $56^1/_2$".

From cream tone-on-tone print:

- Cut 3 *lengthwise* **narrow strips** $5^1/_2$" x $56^1/_2$".

From binding fabric:

- Cut 6 **binding strips** $1^1/_2$" wide.

Cutting the Appliqués

*Follow **Fusible Appliqué**, page 79, to make appliqués from patterns.*

From assorted pink prints:

- Cut 60 **petals** (page 49).

From blue print:

- Cut 15 **berries** (page 58).

From assorted green prints:

- Cut 15 **leaves** (page 58).
- Cut 15 **calyxes** (page 49).

Making the Quilt Top

*Follow **Piecing** and **Pressing**, page 77. Match right sides and use a $1/4$" seam allowance.*

1. Matching long edges, sew 4 **wide strips** and 3 **narrow strips** together to make quilt top.

Quilt Top

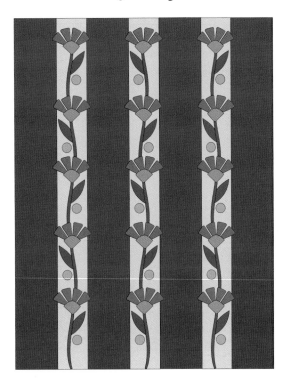

Adding the Appliqués

*Refer to **Blanket Stitch Appliqué**, page 79, for stitching techniques.*

1. Referring to **Continuous Bias Strips**, page 82, use green print **square** to make a 1" wide x 165" long **bias strip**.
2. Using the bias tape maker, follow the manufacturer's instructions to make $1/2$" wide bias tape from bias strip. Cut bias tape into 3 equal length **stems**.
3. Aligning 1 raw end of stem with raw edge of quilt top and trimming remaining end as needed, arrange 1 stem on each narrow strip; secure with drops of basting. Blanket Stitch stems in place.
4. Arrange petals, calyxes, leaves, and berries on narrow strips; fuse. Blanket Stitch around appliqués.

Completing the Quilt

1. Follow **Quilting**, page 80, to mark, layer, and quilt as desired. My quilt is machine quilted with outline quilting around the appliqués and an all-over leaf and swirl pattern on the strips.
2. If desired, follow **Adding A Hanging Sleeve**, page 82, to add a hanging sleeve.
3. Use **binding strips** and follow **Continuous Straight-Grain Strips**, page 84, to make **binding**. Follow **Attaching Binding with Mitered Corners**, page 84, to bind quilt. ❁

In the Pink Leaf
Cut 15

In the Pink Berry
Cut 15

Pear-a-licious

59

This long pillow makes a real statement when displayed on a couch, porch swing, or bed. To get your creative juices flowing, I show it in two colorways, pages 59 and 61. The pear appliqués are from the May block, page 14. And, because the pillow is not a standard size, I have included instructions for the easy-to-make pillow insert.

Finished Size: 29" x 13" (74 cm x 33 cm)

Fabric Requirements

Yardage is based on 43"/44" (109 cm/112 cm) wide fabric with a usable width of 40" (102 cm). Yardage requirements are for 1 pillow and insert.

$16^1/_2$" x $12^1/_2$" (42 cm x 32 cm) rectangle of white solid for center rectangle

$^1/_4$ yd (23 cm) of green/pink print for side rectangles

$^1/_8$ yd (11 cm) of green print for accent strips

Five 5" x 8" (13 cm x 20 cm) rectangles of assorted green and yellow prints for pears and leaf

Scrap of brown print for stems

$^3/_8$ yd (34 cm) of backing fabric

$^1/_4$ yd (23 cm) of binding fabric

1 yd (91 cm) of lightweight muslin

You will also need:

$32^1/_2$" x $16^1/_2$" (83 cm x 42 cm) rectangle of batting

Polyester fiberfill

Paper-backed fusible web

Cutting the Pieces

*Follow **Rotary Cutting**, page 76, to cut fabric. Cut all strips from the selvage-to-selvage width of the fabric. All measurements include $^1/_4$" seam allowances.*

From green/pink print:
- Cut 2 **side rectangles** $5^1/_2$" x $12^1/_2$".

From green print:
- Cut 2 **accent strips** $1^1/_2$" x $12^1/_2$".

From backing fabric:
- Cut 2 **backing rectangles** $18^1/_2$" x $12^1/_2$".

From binding fabric:
- Cut 3 **binding strips** $1^1/_2$" wide.

From muslin:
- Cut 1 **pillow front backing** $32^1/_2$" x $16^1/_2$".
- Cut 2 **insert rectangles** $28^1/_2$" x $12^1/_2$".

Cutting the Appliqués

*Follow **Fusible Appliqué**, page 79, to make appliqués from patterns.*

From green print rectangles:
- Cut 2 **large pears** (page 45).
- Cut 2 **medium pears** (page 45).
- Cut 1 **small pear** (page 45).
- Cut 1 **leaf** (page 46).

From brown scraps:
- Cut 4 **stems A** (page 45).
- Cut 1 **stem B** (page 45).

Making the Pillow

*Follow **Piecing** and **Pressing**, page 77. Match right sides (unless otherwise noted) and use a $^1/_4$" seam allowance. Refer to **Blanket Stitch Appliqué**, page 79, for stitching techniques.*

1. For insert, leave an opening for turning and sew **insert rectangles** together; clip corners.
2. Turn insert right side out; press. Fill with fiberfill and hand sew opening closed.
3. For pillow, match long edges and sew 1 **side rectangle** and 1 **accent strip** together to make **Unit 1**. Make 2 Unit 1's.

Unit 1 (make 2)

4. Sew 1 Unit 1 to each short edge of **center rectangle** to make pillow front.

Pillow Front

5. Placing bottom edges of **pears** $2^{1}/_{2}$"-3" above 1 long raw edge, arrange appliqués on pillow front; fuse.
6. Blanket Stitch around appliqués.
7. Refer to **Quilting**, page 80, to layer and quilt pillow front, batting, and pillow front backing as desired. My pillow is quilted with an all-over loop design.

8. Press 1 short edge of each **backing rectangle** $^{1}/_{4}$" to the wrong side twice; hem.
9. With right sides up, overlap hemmed edges of backing rectangles until piece measures $28^{1}/_{2}$" x $12^{1}/_{2}$". Baste along overlapped edges to make **pillow back** (Fig. 1).

Fig. 1

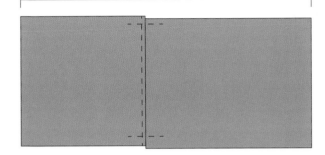

28½"

10. Matching *wrong* sides, layer pillow back and front; pin or baste layers together.
11. Use **binding strips** and follow **Continuous Straight-Grain Strips**, page 84, to make **binding**. Follow **Attaching Binding with Mitered Corners**, page 84, to bind pillow.
12. Place insert in pillow. ❖

Slouchy Project Bag

This is a great travel bag for handwork projects. When you place the bag on your lap, the sides "slouch" open to allow easy access to your project. When it's time to go, just grab both straps and everything is safely contained! The appliqués are from the May block, page 14. For a different look, omit the appliqués and use a fun novelty print for the center panel, page 64.

Finished Size: approximately 22^1/$_2$" x 9^1/$_2$" (57 cm x 24 cm)

Fabric Requirements

Yardage is based on 43"/44" (109 cm/112 cm) wide fabric with a usable width of 40" (102 cm).

- 10" x 10" (26 cm x 26 cm) square of yellow print for **center front**
- ^{3}/$_8$ yd (34 cm) of yellow/pink print for center back, strap accents, and lining
- ^{3}/$_8$ yd (34 cm) of pink print # 1 for outer sides
- ^{1}/$_2$ yd (56 cm) of pink print # 2 for lining, straps, binding, and appliqués
- 8" x 8" (20 cm x 20 cm) square of green print for leaves and stems
- 8" x 8" (20 cm x 20 cm) square of dark green print for flower centers

You will also need:

- 1^1/$_4$ yds (1.1 m) of baby rickrack
- 30" x 30" (76 cm x 76 cm) square of batting
- Paper-backed fusible web

Cutting the Pieces

*Follow **Rotary Cutting**, page 76, to cut fabric. Cut all strips from the selvage-to-selvage width of the fabric. All measurements include ^{1}/$_4$" seam allowances.*

From yellow/pink print:

- Cut 1 strip 10" wide. From this strip, cut 3 **squares** 10" x 10".
- Cut 2 **strap accents** 1^1/$_4$" x 20".

From pink print #1:

- Use side pattern, page 65, to cut 2 **outer sides** and 2 **outer sides reversed**.

From pink print #2:

- Cut 2 **straps** 3" x 20".
- Cut 2 **binding strips** 1^1/$_2$" wide.
- Use side pattern, page 65, to cut 2 **lining sides** and 2 **lining sides reversed**.

From batting:

- Cut 2 **batting straps** 1^1/$_2$" x 20".

Cutting the Appliqués

*Follow **Fusible Appliqué**, page 79, to make appliqués from patterns, pages 45-46 and 65.*

From pink print #2:

- Cut 3 **flowers** (page 45).

From green print:

- Cut 3 **leaves** (page 65).
- Cut 3 **stems** ^{1}/$_2$" x 4^1/$_2$".

From dark green print:

- Cut 3 **star petals** (page 46).

Making the Bag

*Follow **Piecing** and **Pressing**, page 77. Match right sides and use a ^{1}/$_4$" seam allowance. Refer to **Blanket Stitch Appliqué**, page 79, for stitching techniques.*

1. Working from background up, arrange **stems**, **leaves**, **flowers**, and **star petals** on **center front**; fuse.
2. Blanket Stitch around appliqués.
3. Sew 1 **outer side** and 1 **outer side reversed** to opposite sides of center front to make **bag front**.

Bag Front

4. Sew 1 **outer side** and 1 **outer side reversed** to opposite sides of 1 **square** to make **bag back**.
5. Repeat Step 4 using remaining squares, 2 **side linings**, and 2 **side linings reversed** to make 2 **bag linings**.

6. Cut rickrack into 4 equal length pieces. Center and stitch 1 rickrack piece over each seam of bag front. Trim rickrack ends even with raw edges of bag front (**Fig. 1**). Repeat for bag back.

Fig. 1

7. With right sides up, use bag front and bag back as patterns to cut 1 piece of batting 1" larger on all sides than each bag piece.

8. Refer to **Machine Quilting Methods**, page 82, to quilt bag front and back as desired. My bag is outline quilted around each appliqué. There are straight lines spaced approximately $1^{1}/_{2}$" apart on each front side and across the entire bag back. Trim batting even with raw edges of bag front and bag back.

9. Matching wrong sides, sew bag front and bag back together (**Fig. 2**) to make **bag**; turn right side out. Repeat using lining front and back to make **lining**.

Fig. 2

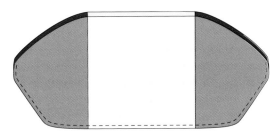

10. Matching wrong sides and top raw edges, slip lining into bag. Baste around top edge (**Fig. 3**).

Fig. 3

11. For straps, press under each long edge of each outer strap $^{1}/_{4}$" to the wrong side. Layer 1 outer strap (wrong side up), 1 strap batting, and 1 strap accent (right side up) as shown in **Fig. 4**.

Fig. 4

Slouchy Bag Side Pattern
Cut 2 outer sides,
2 outer sides reversed,
2 linings, and
2 linings reversed

12. Fold and pin long edges of 1 outer strap ¹/₂" to the wrong side, covering edges of strap accent and strap batting. Topstitch through all layers along each inner folded edge (**Fig. 5**). Repeat using remaining strap, strap accent, and strap batting.

Fig. 5

13. Matching right sides, baste 1 strap to bag front as shown in **Fig. 6**. Repeat to baste remaining strap to bag back.

Fig. 6

Leaf
Cut 3

14. Use **binding strips** and follow **Continuous Straight-Grain Strips**, page 84, to make **binding**.
15. Follow **Binding The Slouchy Project Bag,** page 87, to bind top edge of bag.

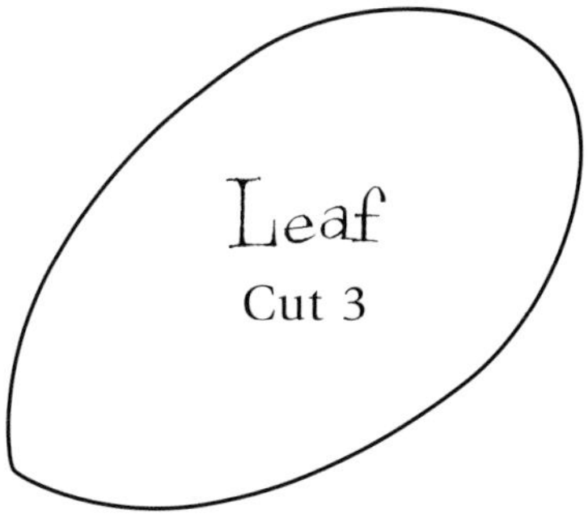

Snow Day

Add a little whimsy to a cold winter day with this fun little quilt. It's the perfect size for a table runner or wall hanging! For the appliqués, I chose the Snowman from the January block, page 6, added the word "Snow," and used spoke-style snowflakes.

Finished Size: 43" x 21" (109 cm x 53 cm)

Fabric Requirements

Yardage is based on 43"/44" (109 cm/112 cm) wide fabric with a usable width of 40" (102 cm).

- $1/2$ yd (57 cm) of light blue print for background
- $1/4$ yd (23 cm) of blue check for inner border and checkerboard border
- $3/8$ yd (34 cm) of dark blue print for background and checkerboard border
- 20" x 5" (51 cm x 13 cm) rectangle of red plaid for hat
- $3/8$ yd (34 cm) *total* of assorted cream and white fabrics for snowman, snowflakes, letters, and pompom
- Scraps of red, orange, and brown prints for remaining appliqués
- $1^3/8$ yds (1.3 m) of backing fabric
- $1/4$ yd (23 cm) of binding fabric

You will also need:
- 5 assorted black buttons for eyes and tummy
- 47" x 25" (119 cm x 64 cm) rectangle of batting
- Template plastic (Needle-Turn Appliqué) **or** paper-backed fusible web (Fusible Appliqué)

Cutting the Pieces

*Follow **Rotary Cutting**, page 76, to cut fabric. Cut all strips from the selvage-to-selvage width of the fabric. All measurements include $1/4$" seam allowances.*

From light blue print:
- Cut 1 strip $15^1/2$" wide. From this strip, cut 4 **large rectangles** $7^1/2$" x $15^1/2$".

From blue check:
- Cut 2 **strips** $2^1/2$" wide.
- Cut 2 **side inner borders** 1" x $15^1/2$".
- Cut 2 **top/bottom inner borders** 1" x $38^1/2$".

From dark blue print:
- Cut 2 **strips** $2^1/2$" wide.
- Cut 2 strips $3^1/2$" wide. From these strips, cut 3 **small rectangles** $3^1/2$" x $15^1/2$".

From binding fabric:
- Cut 4 **binding strips** $1^1/2$" wide.

Cutting the Appliqués

*Follow Steps 1-3 of **Needle-Turn Appliqué**, page 78, to make appliqués from patterns, pages 38-39 and 70. **Note:** If you prefer machine over hand appliqué, follow **Fusible Appliqué**, page 79.*

From cream and white prints:
- Cut 1 **snowman head**.
- Cut 1 **snowman tummy**.
- Cut 1 **snowman base**.
- Cut 9 **snowflake strips** $1/2$" x $8^1/2$".
- Cut the letters **SNOW**.
- Cut 1 **pompom**.

From red plaid:
- Cut 1 **hat**.

From scraps of red, orange, and brown prints:
- Cut 1 **hatband**.
- Cut 1 **nose**.
- Cut 1 **right arm**.
- Cut 1 **left arm**.

Making the Quilt Top

*Follow **Piecing** and **Pressing**, page 77. Match right sides and use a ¹/₄" seam allowance. Refer to **Quilt Top Diagram** to make quilt top.*

1. Matching long edges, sew 4 **large** and 3 **small rectangles** together to make **background**.

2. Matching centers and corners, sew 1 **side inner border** to each short edge of background. Repeat to add **top/ bottom inner borders** to long edges to make **quilt top center**.

3. Referring to **Making Strip Sets**, page 77, use blue check and dark blue **strips** to make 2 **Strip Sets**. From these, cut 30 **Unit 1's**.

Unit 1 (make 30)

2½"

4. Matching short edges and alternating colors, sew 4 Unit 1's together to make **side border**. Make 2 side borders.

Side Border (make 2)

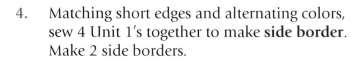

5. Matching short edges and alternating colors, sew 11 Unit 1's together to make **Unit 2**. Make 2 Unit 2's.

Unit 2 (make 2)

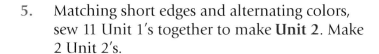

6. Remove 1 blue check square from 1 end of 1 Unit 2 for **top border** and 1 dark blue print square from 1 end of remaining Unit 2 for **bottom border**.

Top Border

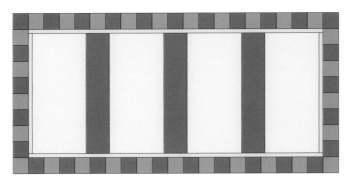

Bottom Border

7. Sew side borders to short edges of quilt top center. Sew top, then bottom border to long edges of quilt top center to complete **quilt top**.

Quilt Top Diagram

Adding the Appliqués

*Refer to Steps 4-8 of **Needle-Turn Appliqué**, page 78, for hand stitching techniques. Refer to **Blanket Stitch Appliqué**, page 79, for machine stitching techniques.*

1. Working from background up, arrange **appliqués** on quilt top.
2. Hand Blindstitch or machine Blanket Stitch around appliqués.
3. Sew 2 buttons to snowman's head and 3 buttons to snowman's tummy.

Completing the Quilt

1. Follow **Quilting**, page 80, to mark, layer, and quilt as desired. My quilt is machine quilted with outline quilting around the appliqués and an all-over swirl pattern in the background. There is a swirl quilted in each block of the border.
2. If desired, follow **Adding A Hanging Sleeve**, page 82, to add a hanging sleeve.
3. Use **binding strips** and follow **Continuous Straight-Grain Strips**, page 84, to make **binding**. Follow **Attaching Binding with Mitered Corners**, page 84, to bind quilt.

Moon Flowers

This cheerful table set is a snap to make. For the appliqués, I used the Moonflowers from the September block, page 22, and arranged them around a wreath for the table mat. Each coordinating placemat features a single bloom.

Table Mat Finished Size: 27" x 27" (69 cm x 69 cm)
Placemat Finished Size: 19" x 11" (48 cm x 28 cm)

Fabric Requirements

Yardage is based on 43"/44" (109 cm/112 cm) wide fabric with a usable width of 40" (102 cm). Yardages given are for 1 table mat and 2 placemats.

- 18$^1/_2$" x 18$^1/_2$" (47 cm x 47 cm) square of cream print for table mat center square
- $^3/_8$ yd (34 cm) of dark blue print for table mat
- $^1/_4$ yd (23 cm) of light blue print for table mat
- $^3/_8$ yd (34 cm) *each* of 2 blue floral prints for table mat and placemats
- $^1/_4$ yd (23 cm) of tan print for placemats
- $^1/_4$ yd (23 cm) of green print for placemats, leaves, and calyxes.
- $^1/_4$ yd (23 cm) of dark green print for wreath and stems.
- 5" x 15" (13 cm x 38 cm) rectangle of orange print for placemats
- 10" x 15" (25 cm x 38 cm) rectangle of yellow print for placemats
- 1$^1/_2$ yds (1.4 m) of backing fabric
- $^3/_8$ yd (34 cm) of binding fabric

You will also need:

- 31" x 31" (79 cm x 79 cm) square of batting for table topper
- 15" x 23" (38 cm x 137 cm) rectangle of batting for placemats
- Paper-backed fusible web

Cutting the Pieces

*Follow **Rotary Cutting**, page 76, to cut fabric. Cut all strips from the selvage-to-selvage width of the fabric. All measurements include $^1/_4$" seam allowances.*

From dark blue print:
- Cut 2 strips 4$^1/_2$" wide. From these strips, cut 8 **small squares** 4$^1/_2$" x 4$^1/_2$" and 4 **small rectangles** 4$^1/_2$" x 2$^1/_2$".
- Cut 2 **large squares** 5" x 5".

From light blue print:
- Cut 1 strip 5" wide. From this strip, cut 2 **large squares** 5" x 5" and 4 **small squares** 4$^1/_2$" x 4$^1/_2$".

From 1 blue floral print:
- Cut 1 strip 8$^1/_2$" wide. From this strip, cut 8 **medium rectangles** 8$^1/_2$" x 4$^1/_2$".

From remaining blue floral print:
- Cut 1 strip 10$^1/_2$" wide. From this strip, cut 2 **extra-large rectangles** 10$^1/_2$" x 12$^1/_2$".

From tan print:
- Cut 2 **large rectangles** 5$^1/_2$" x 10$^1/_2$".

From green print:
- Cut 2 **sashing strips** 1$^1/_2$" x 10$^1/_2$".

From backing fabric:
- Cut 1 **table mat backing** 31" x 31".
- Cut 2 **placemat backings** 15" x 23".

From binding fabric:
- Cut 3 **table mat binding strips** 1$^1/_2$" wide.
- Cut 4 **placemat binding strips** 1$^1/_2$" wide.

Cutting the Appliqués

*Follow **Fusible Appliqué**, page 79, to make appliqués from patterns, pages 50 and 75.*

From green print:
- Cut 8 **leaves**.
- Cut 8 **calyxes**.

From dark green print:
- Cut 1 **wreath**.
- Cut 2 **stems** $^1/_2$" x 5$^1/_2$".

From yellow print:
- Cut 3 **flowers**.

From orange print:
- Cut 5 **flowers**.

Making the Table Set

*Follow **Piecing** and **Pressing**, page 77. Match right sides and use a 1/4" seam allowance.*

TABLE MAT

1. Draw a diagonal line on the wrong side of each light blue **small square**. Place 1 small square on each corner of the table mat center square. Sew on drawn line; trim 1/4" from stitching line (**Fig. 1**). Press open to make **table mat center**.

Fig. 1

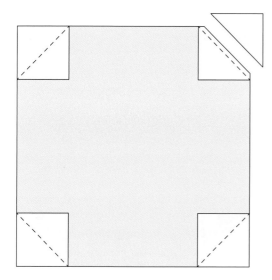

Table Mat Center

2. Draw a diagonal line on wrong side of each light blue **large square**.

3. Matching right sides and aligning corners, place 1 marked large square on top of 1 dark blue **large square**. Stitch 1/4" from each side of drawn line (**Fig. 2**). Cut along drawn line and press seam allowances toward darker fabric to make 2 **Triangle-Squares**. Trim each Triangle-Square to 4 1/2" x 4 1/2". Make 4 Triangle-Squares.

Fig. 2

Triangle-Square (make 4)

4. Draw a diagonal line on the wrong side of each dark blue **small square**. Place 1 marked small square on left corner of 1 floral **medium rectangle**. Sew on drawn line; trim 1/4" from stitching line (**Fig. 3**). Press open to make **Unit 1**. Make 4 Unit 1's.

Fig. 3

Unit 1 (make 4)

5. Placing small squares on right corner of medium rectangles, repeat Step 4 to make 4 **Unit 2's**.

Unit 2 (make 4)

6. Sew 1 Unit, 1 **small rectangle**, and 1 Unit 2 together to make border. Make 4 borders.

Border (make 4)

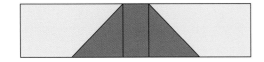

7. Sew 1 border to opposite sides of table mat center to make Unit 3.

Unit 3

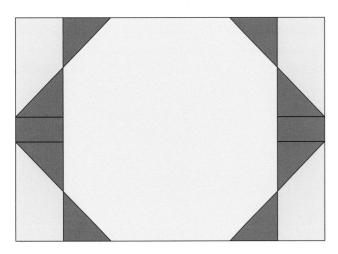

8. Sew 1 Triangle-Square to each end of remaining borders to make Unit 4. Make 2 Unit 4's.

Unit 4 (make 2)

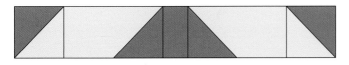

9. Sew 1 Unit 4 to remaining sides of Unit 3 to make **table mat top**.

Table Mat Top

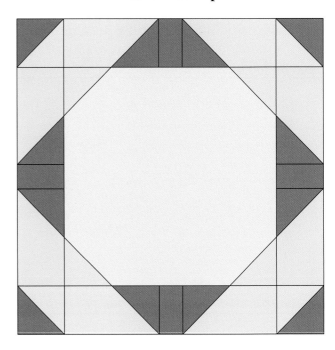

PLACEMATS

1. Matching $10^{1}/_{2}$" edges, sew 1 **large rectangle**, 1 **sashing strip**, and 1 **extra-large rectangle** together to make placemat top. Make 2 placemat tops.

Placemat Top (make 2)

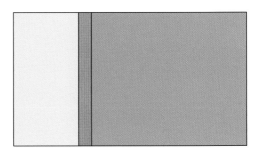

Adding the Appliqués

*Refer to **Blanket Stitch Appliqué**, page 79, for stitching techniques.*

TABLE MAT

1. Center and fuse **wreath** on table mat top. Blanket Stitch around wreath.
2. Working from background up, arrange 3 yellow **flowers**, 3 orange **flowers**, 6 **calyxes**, and 6 **leaves** on table mat top; fuse.
3. Blanket Stitch around appliqués.

PLACEMATS

1. Working from background up, arrange 1 **stem**, 1 **flower**, 1 **calyx**, and 1 **leaf** on placemat top; fuse.
2. Blanket Stitch around appliqués.
3. Repeat Steps 1-2 for remaining placemat.

Completing the Table Set

1. Follow **Quilting**, page 80, to mark, layer, and quilt the table set as desired. My table mat is machine quilted with outline quilting around the appliqués and center square. There is a swirling leaf in the center of the wreath and a loop design in the remainder of the center square. My placemats have outline quilting around the appliqués and a loop design across the remainder of the placemat.
2. If desired, follow **Adding A Hanging Sleeve**, page 82, to add a hanging sleeve.
3. Use **binding strips** and follow **Continuous Straight-Grain Strips**, page 84, to make **binding**. Follow **Attaching Binding with Mitered Corners**, page 84, to bind each piece of the table set. ❁

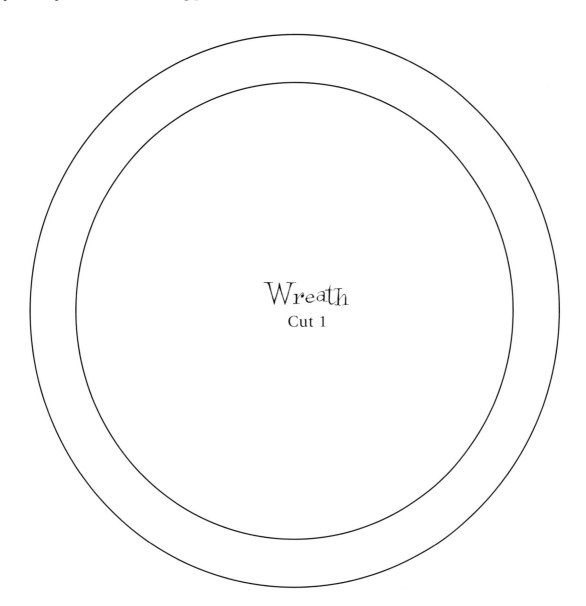

Wreath
Cut 1

General Instructions

To make your quilting easier and more enjoyable, carefully read all of the general instructions, study the color photographs, and familiarize yourself with the individual project instructions before beginning a project.

Rotary Cutting

- Place fabric on work surface with fold closest to you.

- Cut all strips from the selvage-to-selvage width of the fabric unless otherwise indicated in project instructions.

- Square left edge of fabric using rotary cutter and rulers (Figs. 1-2).

Fig. 1	Fig. 2

- To cut each strip required for a project, place ruler over cut edge of fabric, aligning desired marking on ruler with cut edge; make cut (Fig. 3).

Fig. 3

- When cutting several strips from a single piece of fabric, it is important to make sure that cuts remain at a perfect right angle to the fold; square fabric as needed.

Piecing

Precise cutting, followed by accurate piecing, will ensure that all pieces of the quilt top fit together well.

- Set sewing machine stitch length for approximately 11 stitches per inch.

- Use neutral-colored general-purpose sewing thread (not quilting thread) in the needle and bobbin.

- An accurate $1/4$" seam allowance is *essential*. Presser feet that are $1/4$" wide are available for most sewing machines.

- When piecing, always place pieces right sides together and match raw edges; pin if necessary.

- Chain piecing saves time and will usually result in more accurate piecing.

- Trim away points of seam allowances that extend beyond edges of sewn pieces.

Making Strip Sets

Matching long edges, sew 1 cream print and 1 black print strip together to make 1 **Strip Set**. Make the number of Strip Sets indicated in project instructions. Cut across the Strip Sets at $2^1/2$" intervals to make the number of **Unit 1's** indicated in project instructions.

Strip Set   **Unit 1**

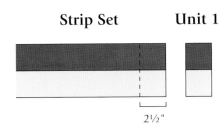

2½"

Sewing Across Seam Intersections

When sewing across the intersection of two seams, place pieces right sides together and match seams exactly, making sure seam allowances are pressed in opposite directions (Fig. 4).

Fig. 4

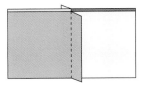

Sewing Sharp Points

To ensure sharp points when joining triangular or diagonal pieces, stitch across the center of the "X" (shown in pink) formed on wrong side by previous seams (Fig. 5).

Fig. 5

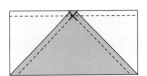

Pressing

- Use steam iron set on "Cotton" for all pressing.

- Press after sewing each seam.

- Seam allowances are almost always pressed to one side, usually toward darker fabric. However, to reduce bulk it may occasionally be necessary to press seam allowances toward the lighter fabric or even to press them open.

- To prevent dark fabric seam allowance from showing through light fabric, trim darker seam allowance slightly narrower than lighter seam allowance.

- To press long seams, such as those in long strip sets, without curving or other distortion, lay strips across width of the ironing board.

Needle-Turn Appliqué

Using a needle to turn under the seam allowance while blindstitching an appliqué to background fabric is called "needle-turn appliqué."

1. To make a template from a pattern, use a permanent fine-point pen and a ruler to carefully trace the pattern onto template plastic. Cut out template along inner edge of drawn line. **Note:** Patterns are printed in reverse. Turn templates over and mark the right side.

2. Place template, right side up, on right side of appliqué fabric. Lightly draw around template with pencil, leaving at least $^1/_2$" between shapes. Repeat for number of shapes specified in project instructions.

3. Cut out shapes approximately $^3/_{16}$" outside drawn line. Clip inside curves and points up to, but not through, drawn line.

4. Arrange shapes on background fabric and pin or baste in place. Thread a sharps needle with a single strand of general-purpose sewing thread that matches appliqué; knot one end.

5. Begin blindstitching on as straight an edge as possible, turning a small section of seam allowance to wrong side with the tip of the needle, concealing drawn line (Fig. 6).

Fig. 6

6. To stitch outward points, stitch to $^1/_2$" from point (Fig. 7). Turn seam allowance under at point (Fig. 8); then turn remainder of seam allowance between stitching and point. Stitch to point, taking two or three stitches at top of point to secure. Turn under small amount of seam allowance past point and resume stitching.

Fig. 7   **Fig. 8**

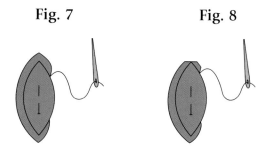

7. To stitch inward point, stitch to $^1/_2$" from point (Fig. 9). Clip to but not through seam allowance at point (Fig. 10). Turn seam allowance under between stitching and point. Stitch to point, taking two or three stitches at point to secure. Turn under small amount of seam allowance past point and resume stitching.

Fig. 9   **Fig. 10**

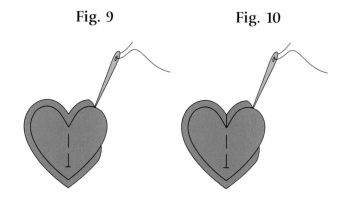

8. Do not turn under or stitch seam allowances that will be covered by other appliqué pieces.

Fusible Appliqué

Applique patterns are printed in reverse to enable you to use our speedy method of preparing appliqué shapes.

1. Place paper-backed fusible web, paper side up, over appliqué pattern. Trace pattern onto paper side of web with pencil as many times as indicated in project instructions for a single fabric.

2. Follow manufacturer's instructions to fuse traced patterns to wrong side of fabrics. Do not remove paper backing. (**Note:** Some pieces may be given as measurements, such as a 2" x 4" rectangle, instead of drawn patterns. Fuse web to wrong side of fabrics indicated for these pieces.)

3. Use scissors to cut out appliqué pieces along traced lines; use rotary cutting equipment to cut out appliqué pieces given as measurements. Remove paper backing from all pieces.

Blanket Stitch Appliqué

Some machines have feature a Blanket Stitch similar to the one used in this book. Refer to your owner's manual to set-up machine. If your machine does not have this stitch, try any of the decorative stitches your machine has until you are satisfied with the look.

1. If desired, pin stabilizer, such as paper or any of the commercially available products, on wrong side of background fabric or spray the wrong side of background fabric with starch.

2. Thread sewing machine with general-purpose thread; use general-purpose thread that matches background fabric in bobbin.

3. Set sewing machine for a medium (approximately $1/8$") stitch width and a short stitch length. Slightly loosening the top tension may yield a smoother stitch.

4. Begin by stitching two or three stitches in place (drop feed dogs or set stitch length at 0) to anchor thread. Most of the stitch should be on the appliqué with the right edge of the stitch falling at the outside edge of the appliqué. Stitch over all exposed raw edges of appliqué pieces.

5. (**Note:** Dots on **Figs. 11-15** indicate where to leave needle in fabric when pivoting.) For outside corners, stitch just past corner, stopping with needle in background fabric (Fig. 11). Raise presser foot. Pivot project, lower presser foot, and stitch adjacent side (Fig. 12).

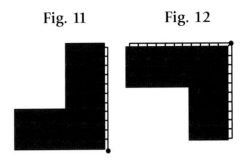

Fig. 11   **Fig. 12**

6. For inside corners, stitch just past corner, stopping with needle in background fabric (Fig. 13). Raise presser foot. Pivot project, lower presser foot, and stitch adjacent side (Fig. 14).

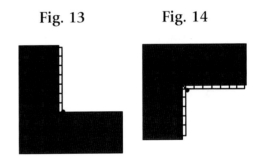

Fig. 13   **Fig. 14**

7. When stitching outside curves, stop with needle in background fabric. Raise presser foot and pivot project as needed. Lower presser foot and continue stitching, pivoting as often as necessary to follow curve (Fig. 15).

Fig. 15

8. When stitching inside curves, stop with needle in background fabric. Raise presser foot and pivot project as needed. Lower presser foot and continue stitching, pivoting as often as necessary to follow curve (Fig. 16).

Fig. 16

9. Do not backstitch at end of stitching. Pull threads to wrong side of background fabric; knot thread and trim ends.
10. Carefully tear away stabilizer.

Quilting

*Quilting holds the three layers (top, batting, and backing) of the quilt together and can be done by hand or machine. Because marking, layering, and quilting are interrelated and may be done in different orders depending on circumstances, please read entire **Quilting** section, pages 80-82, before beginning project.*

Marking Quilting Lines

Quilting lines may be marked using fabric marking pencils, chalk markers, or water- or air-soluble pens.

Simple quilting designs may be marked with chalk or chalk pencil after basting. A small area may be marked, then quilted, before moving to next area to be marked. Intricate designs should be marked before basting using a more durable marker.

Caution: Pressing may permanently set some marks. **Test** different markers **on scrap fabric** to find one that marks clearly and can be thoroughly removed.

A wide variety of pre-cut quilting stencils, as well as entire books of quilting patterns, are available. Using a stencil makes it easier to mark intricate or repetitive designs.

To make a stencil from a pattern, center template plastic over pattern and use a permanent marker to trace pattern onto plastic. Use a craft knife with single or double blade to cut channels along traced lines (Fig. 17).

Fig. 17

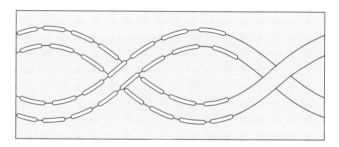

Preparing the Backing

To allow for a slight shifting during quilting, the backing should be approximately 4" larger on all sides than the quilt top. Yardage requirements listed for quilt backings are calculated for 43"/44"w fabric. Using 90"w or 108"w fabric for the backing of a bed-sized quilt may eliminate piecing. To piece a backing using 43"/44"w fabric, use the following instructions.

1. Measure length and width of quilt top; add 8" to each measurement.

2. If determined width is 79" or less, cut backing fabric into two lengths slightly longer than determined *length* measurement. Trim selvages. Place lengths with right sides facing and sew long edges together, forming a tube (Fig. 18). Match seams and press along one fold (Fig. 19). Cut along pressed fold to form a single piece (Fig. 20).

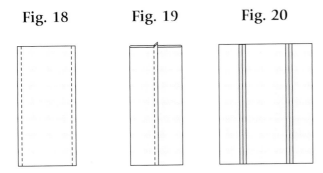

Fig. 18 **Fig. 19** **Fig. 20**

3. If determined width is more than 79", it may require less fabric yardage if the backing is pieced horizontally. Divide determined *length* measurement by 40" to determine how many widths will be needed. Cut required number of widths the determined *width* measurement. Trim selvages. Sew long edges together to form single piece.

4. Trim backing to size determined in Step 1; press seam allowances open.

Choosing the Batting

The appropriate batting will make quilting easier. For fine hand quilting, choose low-loft batting. All cotton or cotton/polyester blend battings work well for machine quilting because the cotton helps "grip" quilt layers. If quilt is to be tied, a high-loft batting, sometimes called extra-loft or fat batting, may be used to make quilt "fluffy."

Types of batting include cotton, polyester, wool, cotton/polyester blend, cotton/wool blend, and silk.

When selecting batting, refer to package labels for characteristics and care instructions. Cut batting same size as prepared backing.

Assembling the Quilt

1. Examine wrong side of quilt top closely; trim any seam allowances and clip any threads that may show through front of the quilt. Press quilt top, being careful not to "set" any marked quilting lines.

2. Place backing *wrong* side up on flat surface. Use masking tape to tape edges of backing to surface. Place batting on top of backing fabric. Smooth batting gently, being careful not to stretch or tear. Center quilt top *right* side up on batting.

3. Use 1" rustproof safety pins to "pin-baste" all layers together, spacing pins approximately 4" apart. Begin at center and work toward outer edges to secure all layers. If possible, place pins away from areas that will be quilted, although pins may be removed as needed when quilting.

Machine Quilting Methods

Use general-purpose thread in bobbin. Do not use quilting thread. Thread the needle of machine with general-purpose thread or transparent monofilament thread to make quilting blend with quilt top fabrics. Use decorative thread, such as a metallic or contrasting-color general-purpose thread, to make quilting lines stand out more.

Straight-Line Quilting
The term "straight-line" is somewhat deceptive, since curves (especially gentle ones) as well as straight lines can be stitched with this technique.

1. Set stitch length for six to ten stitches per inch and attach a walking foot to the sewing machine.

2. Determine which section of quilt will have longest continuous quilting line, oftentimes the area from the center top to the center bottom. Roll up and secure each edge of the quilt to help reduce the bulk, keeping fabrics smooth. Smaller projects may not need to be rolled.

3. Begin stitching on the longest quilting line, using very short stitches for the first $1/4$" to "lock" quilting. Stitch across project, using one hand on each side of walking foot to slightly spread fabric and to guide fabric through machine. Lock stitches at end of quilting line.

4. Continue machine quilting, stitching longer quilting lines first to stabilize quilt before moving on to other areas.

Free-Motion Quilting

Free-motion quilting allows you to move the quilt in any direction under the needle letting you make loops, swirls flowers, leaves, vines and other shapes. This type of quilting may be free form or may follow a marked pattern.

1. Attach darning foot to sewing machine and lower or cover feed dogs.

2. Position quilt under darning foot; lower foot. Holding top thread, take a stitch and pull bobbin thread to top of quilt. To "lock" beginning of quilting line, hold top and bobbin threads while making three to five stitches in place.

3. Use one hand on each side of darning foot to slightly spread fabric and to move fabric through the machine. Even stitch length is achieved by using smooth, flowing hand motion and steady machine speed. Slow machine speed and fast hand movement will create long stitches. Fast machine speed and slow hand movement will create short stitches. Move quilt sideways, back and forth, in a circular motion, or in a random motion to create desired designs; do not rotate quilt. Lock stitches at end of each quilting line.

Adding a Hanging Sleeve

Attaching a hanging sleeve to back of wall hanging or quilt before the binding is added allows project to be displayed on wall.

1. Measure width of quilt top edge and subtract 1". Cut piece of fabric 7"w by determined measurement.

2. Press short edges of fabric piece $1/4$" to wrong side; press edges $1/4$" to wrong side again and machine stitch in place.

3. Matching wrong sides, fold piece in half lengthwise to form a tube.

4. Before sewing binding to quilt top, match raw edges and pin hanging sleeve to center top edge on back of quilt; stitch in place.

5. Bind quilt, treating hanging sleeve as part of backing.

6. Blindstitch bottom of hanging sleeve to backing, taking care not to stitch through to front of quilt.

Making Continuous Strips

Continuous Bias Strips

Bias strips for binding or appliqué can simply be cut and pieced to desired length. However, when a long length is needed, the "continuous" method is quick and accurate.

1. Cut **square** (size specified in project instructions) in half diagonally to make two triangles.

2. With right sides together and using $1/4$" seam allowance, sew triangles together (**Fig. 21**); press seam allowances open.

Fig. 21

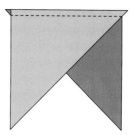

3. On wrong side of fabric, draw lines 2¼" apart (Fig. 22). Cut off any remaining fabric less than this width.

Fig. 22

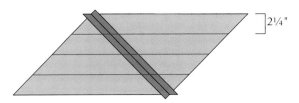

4. With right sides inside, bring short edges together to form tube; match raw edges so that first drawn line of top section meets second drawn line of bottom section (Fig. 23).

Fig. 23

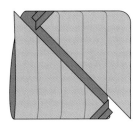

5. Carefully pin edges together by inserting pins through drawn lines at point where drawn lines intersect, making sure pins go through intersections on both sides. Using ¼" seam allowance, sew edges together; press seam allowances open.

6. To cut continuous strip, begin cutting along first drawn line (Fig. 24). Continue cutting along drawn line around tube.

Fig. 24

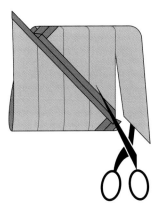

7. Trim ends of bias strip square.
8. For **binding**, press 1 long edge of bias strip ¼" to the wrong side.
   For **vine or stems for appliqué**, follow project instructions.

Continuous Straight-Grain Strips

1. Refer to **Fig. 25** to sew binding strips together using the diagonal seams method.

Fig. 25

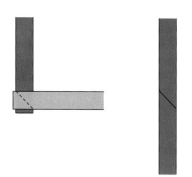

2. For **binding**, press one long edge of strip $^1/_4$" to the wrong side.

Pat's Machine-Sewn Binding

For a quick and easy finish Pat sews her binding to the back of the quilt and Machine Blanket Stitches or Straight Stitches it in place on the front, eliminating all hand stitching.

Attaching Binding with Mitered Corners

1. Using a narrow zigzag, stitch around quilt close to the raw edges (**Fig. 26**). Trim backing and batting even with edges of quilt.

Fig. 26

2. Beginning with one end near center on bottom edge of quilt, lay binding around quilt to make sure that seams in binding will not end up at a corner. Adjust placement if necessary. Matching raw edges of binding to raw edge of quilt top, pin binding to backing side of quilt along one edge.

3. When you reach first corner, mark $^1/_4$" from corner of quilt top (**Fig. 27**).

Fig. 27

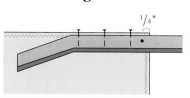

4. Beginning approximately 10" from end of binding and using a $^1/_4$" seam allowance, sew binding to quilt, backstitching at beginning of stitching and at mark (**Fig. 28**). Lift needle out of fabric and clip thread.

Fig. 28

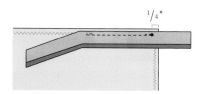

5. Fold binding as shown in **Figs. 29–30** and pin binding to adjacent side, matching raw edges. When you've reached the next corner, mark $^1/_4$" from edge of quilt top.

Fig. 29   **Fig. 30**

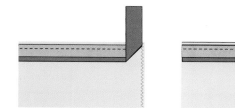

6. Backstitching at edge of quilt top, sew pinned binding to quilt (Fig. 31); backstitch at the next mark. Lift needle out of fabric and clip thread.

Fig. 31

7. Continue sewing binding to quilt, stopping approximately 10" from starting point (Fig. 32).

Fig. 32

8. Bring beginning and end of binding to center of opening and fold each end back, leaving a ¹/₄" space between folds (Fig. 33). Finger press folds.

Fig. 33

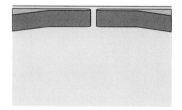

9. Unfold ends of binding and draw a line across wrong side in finger-pressed crease. Draw a line through the lengthwise pressed fold of binding at the same spot to create a cross mark. With edge of ruler at cross mark, line up 45° angle marking on ruler with one long side of binding. Draw a diagonal line from edge to edge. Repeat on remaining end, making sure that the two diagonal lines are angled the same way (Fig. 34).

Fig. 34

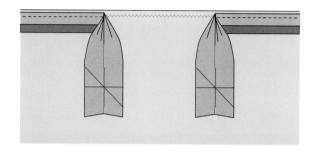

10. Matching right sides and diagonal lines, pin binding ends together at right angles (Fig. 35).

Fig. 35

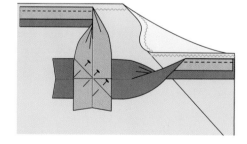

11. Machine stitch along diagonal line (**Fig. 36**), removing pins as you stitch.

Fig. 36

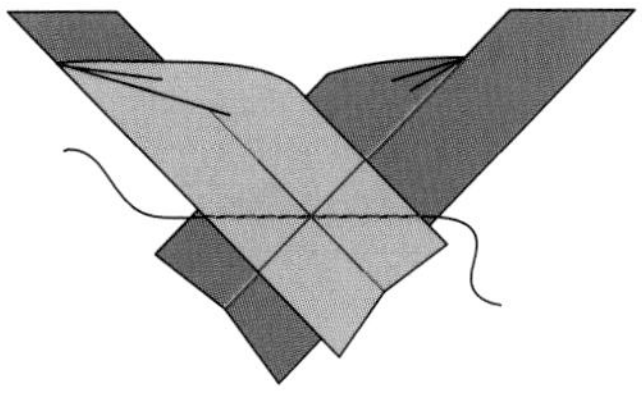

12. Lay binding against quilt to double check that it is correct length.
13. Trim binding ends, leaving $1/4$" seam allowance; press seam open. Stitch binding to quilt.
14. On one edge of quilt, fold binding over to quilt front and pin pressed edge in place, covering stitching line (**Fig. 37**). On adjacent side, fold binding over, forming a mitered corner (**Fig. 38**). Repeat to pin remainder of binding in place.

Fig. 37   **Fig. 38**

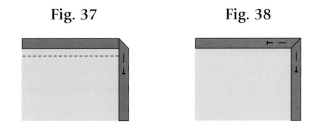

15. Blanket or Straight Stitch folded edge of binding to quilt front.

Attaching Binding with Overlapped Corners

1. Using a narrow zigzag, stitch around quilt close to the raw edges (see **Fig. 26**, page 84). Trim backing and batting even with edges of quilt top.
2. Matching raw edges and using $1/4$" seam allowance, sew a length of binding to top and bottom edges on wrong side of quilt.
3. Trim ends of top and bottom binding even with edges of quilt top. Fold binding over to quilt front and pin pressed edges in place, covering stitching line (**Fig. 39**); Machine Blanket or Straight Stitch binding to quilt front.

Fig. 39

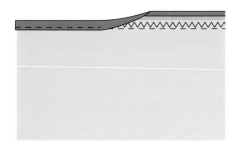

4. Leaving approximately $1^1/2$" of binding at each end, stitch a length of binding to each side edge of quilt (**Fig. 40**).

Fig. 40

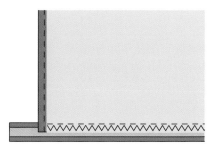

5. Trim each end of binding ¹/₂" longer than bound edge. Fold each end of binding over to quilt front (Fig. 41); pin in place. Fold binding over to quilt front and Machine Blanket or Straight Stitch in place.

Fig. 41

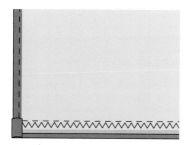

Binding the Slouchy Project Bag

1. Press 1 end of **continuous binding** strip diagonally (Fig. 42)

Fig. 42

2. Beginning on wrong (lining) side of bag with diagonal of binding, match raw edges and pin binding around top edge of bag.
3. Using a ¹/₄" seam allowance, sew binding to bag until binding overlaps the beginning end by about 2".
4. Fold binding to the right side, covering stitching line: pin in place.
5. Machine Blanket or Straight Stitch binding in place close to folded edge.

Signing and Dating Your Quilt

A completed quilt is a work of art and should be signed and dated. There are many different ways to do this and numerous books on the subject. The label should reflect the style of the quilt, the occasion or person for which it was made, and the quilter's own particular talents. Following are suggestions for recording the history of quilt or adding a sentiment for future generations.

- Embroider the quilter's name, date, and any additional information on the quilt top or backing. Matching floss, such as cream floss on white border, will leave a subtle record. Bright or contrasting floss will make the information stand out.

- Make a label from muslin and use a permanent marker to write the information. Use different colored permanent markers to make the label more decorative. Stitch the label to the back of the quilt.

- Use photo-transfer paper to add an image to a white or cream fabric label. Stitch the label to the back of the quilt.

- Write a message on appliquéd design from the quilt top. Attach the appliqué to the back of the quilt.

Caring for Your Quilt

- Wash the finished quilt in cold water on a gentle cycle with mild soap. Soaps such as Orvus® Paste or Charlie's Soap®, which have no softeners, fragrances, whiteners, or other additives are safest. Rinse twice in cold water.

- Use a dye magnet such as Shout® Color Catcher® each time the quilt is washed to absorb any dyes that bled. When washing a quilt for the first time, you may chose to use two dye magnets for extra caution.

- Dry the quilt on low heat/air fluff in 15 minute increments until dry.

Metric Conversion Chart	
Inches x 2.54 = centimeters (cm)	Yards x .9144 = meters (m)
Inches x 25.4 = millimeters (mm)	Yards x 91.44 = centimeters (cm)
Inches x .0254 = meters (m)	Centimeters x .3937 = inches (")
	Meters x 1.0936 = yards (yd)

Standard Equivalents					
1/8"	3.2 mm	0.32 cm	1/8 yard	11.43 cm	0.11 m
1/4"	6.35 mm	0.635 cm	1/4 yard	22.86 cm	0.23 m
3/8"	9.5 mm	0.95 cm	3/8 yard	34.29 cm	0.34 m
1/2"	12.7 mm	1.27 cm	1/2 yard	45.72 cm	0.46 m
5/8"	15.9 mm	1.59 cm	5/8 yard	57.15 cm	0.57 m
3/4"	19.1 mm	1.91 cm	3/4 yard	68.58 cm	0.69 m
7/8"	22.2 mm	2.22 cm	7/8 yard	80 cm	0.8 m
1"	25.4 mm	2.54 cm	1 yard	91.44 cm	0.91 m

Thanks to Cindy Dickinson and JoAnn Hoffman for their beautiful machine quilting.

Thank you to Moda Fabrics, Timeless Treasures, and P&B Textiles for many of the beautiful fabrics featured in these projects and to Bernina for providing my sewing machine. To make the projects I used Aurifil® thread and Warm and Natural® batting.